Richard &Famous

20 years of meeting & snapping the stars

Richard Simpkin

NEW HOLLAND

First published in Australia in 2007 by
New Holland Publishers (Australia) Pty Ltd
Sydney • Auckland • London • Cape Town
Unit 1, 66 Gibbes Street, Chatswood NSW 2067 Australia • 218 Lake Road
Northcoate Auckland New Zealand • New Edgeware Road London W2 2EA
United Kingdom • 80 McKenzie Street Cape Town 8001 South Africa
Copyright © 2007 in text and photographs: Richard Simpkin
Copyright © 2007 New Holland Publishers (Australia) Pty Ltd

A record of this book is held at the National Library of Australia

ISBN 9781741105193

Publisher: Fiona Schultz
Designer: Hayley Norman
Production: Linda Bottari
Printed and bound in Malaysia by Imago Productions

Dedication

To Michael Hutchence, a true 'shining star'

Contents

Introduction

Yesterday I was in my local bookstore which also sells a wide variety of magazines. As I walked through the seven aisles that were mostly filled with celebrity magazines I was amazed at just how many people were fixated on them. All I could hear were girls speaking about how fat someone looks, how skinny another celebrity looks and oh my god is Brad Pitt really going out with her? It's amazing how we as a society are totally obsessed in the lives of celebrities. It was only about fifteen years ago that most women's magazines were filled with cooking recipes and nice stories about everyday people.

Today, like it or not, we live in a celebrity-saturated world, which got me thinking, is celebrity bigger than religion, or is it just far more glamorous? Either way, I think there are far more people around the world right now reading about a celebrity, than there are reading the Bible. Was John Lennon right when in 1966 he said in an interview that 'We (The Beatles) are more popular than Jesus.' Were they, or are they, bigger than Jesus? Or are celebrity gossip magazines the new Bible? Are the movie theatres and concert stages the new churches? What's going on here and how did I get myself so involved? Oh my god! Or should I say 'Oh my celebrity'!

From a very young age I knew that I wanted to become a photographer. Like many people I was interested in celebrities and as a kid I would imagine what it would be like to meet a celebrity and take their photo. The closest thing that I ever came to meeting celebrities was collecting autographs of football players after the game, but in 1988 when I was fifteen I got thinking, if I can meet football players then why can't I meet international celebrities?

In 1988 British pop group Bros were in Sydney to play some concerts. I asked my mum if we could try to meet them. The only question was how and where. The next day my mum drove me around Sydney's five star hotels. I would get out and ask the doorman if Bros were staying at their hotel. After several hotels I was told to go to the Southern Cross Hotel. When I finally ended up there I was told by the doorman that Bros had checked out about three hours ago. He also told me that there had been about 30 screaming girls outside the hotel everyday waiting. 'Did they meet them?' I asked. 'Yes' replied the doorman, he told me that the girls got their autographs and photos everyday. He then went onto tell me that most of the celebrities stayed at a hotel called the Sebel Townhouse.

In 1989 my friend showed me a photo of her father with John Lennon and Yoko Ono taken in the 1970s in New York's Central Park. I remember thinking that that photo was priceless and it captured a moment in time. In 1989 a number of celebrities visited Australia. I remembered what the doorman had told me, so when the rock band Poison came to Sydney I went down to the Sebel and saw about 50 girls and a few guys waiting outside the hotel for the band to come out. After a few days I had met all four members of Poison and got them to sign a poster for me. That year I also met Bon Jovi, Cyndi Lauper, Kylie Minogue, Debbie Gibson, Sammy Davis Jr, U2 and INXS to name but a few.

In January 1990 I bought a $90 camera and decided that I would take photos of celebrities. At the age of sixteen I knew that the celebrities wouldn't come to me for a photoshoot, so I simply went to them. At the time my friends were out chasing girls, I too was chasing girls, except the girls that I was chasing were Kylie Minogue, Cyndi Lauper and Christie Brinkley, but unlike most of my friends I got my girls. Well I got their autograph or photo! I went to hotels, airports, press conferences, celebrity 'hangouts', award ceremonies and sometimes backstage at their concerts. As the years went on I practised my photography skills on these celebrities.

I started to get my photo taken with almost every celebrity that I met. For me getting a photo with a celebrity is far more important than getting their autograph because anyone can buy an autograph but how do you put a price on actually meeting someone that is going to be remembered in history? The Nelson Mandela and Audrey Hepburn photos are a great example. I soon realised that I could mix the ordinary (me) with the extraordinary (the celebrity). I committed myself to getting my photograph next to those that were going to be remembered in history—you might say it's a snapshot or a single person's kaleidoscope of celebrities from the 20th and the 21st centuries. It's a mix and match of two worlds. From my world which is the ordinary to the extraordinary world of the celebrity.

In 1991 I decided that I should concentrate more on taking photos of celebrities rather than getting my photo with them, so for the next couple of years I regrettably only got a handful of photos with the celebrities that I had met.

As the next couple of years passed, people wanted to talk to me about celebrities—every party I went to people would introduce me saying: 'This is Richard, he photographs and meets celebrities.' I could never escape the topic and at the end of the party I was always surrounded by a group of people asking me who I had met, what they were like and could they come with me next time to meet someone that they liked. For a few years it would really bother me that people only wanted to talk to me about celebrities.

Then in 1995 I got thinking, if people were so fascinated in celebrities then I should start to get my photo taken with every celebrity that I met, just like I used to do. It was around this time that I decided to be an artist; though I always thought photography was art I wanted to do something different.

I've always believed that we need to reinvent ourselves and I decided that I was going to build my collection of photos of me with celebrities to the extent that I would look at my collection as art. You see you can take a photo of anyone and that photo is just a photo of a single person, celebrity or not. But as soon as you put someone else in the photo it changes the whole dynamic of that photo. Suddenly it's not all about the celebrity, in a strange way it's about you. Think about it, you'll look at the photo of a celebrity and OK there he or she is, but then you may wonder, how did this everyday person end up in the photo? And this is where the saying 'A picture is worth a thousand words' makes so much sense.

The general public thinks that most celebrities are untouchable and that you simply cannot meet them. Once you see a photo of a celebrity with a non celebrity you begin to ask the questions; how did you meet them, where did you meet them and what were they like? I think that fan photos of celebrities are usually the most interesting photos, because they are real photos of celebrities. They haven't been set up by their management, PRs or PAs. There are no glitzy lights, makeup artists or props in these photos and they are not photos that have been touched up so much that they begin to look more like a painting than a photo!

The photos that I have taken represent a moment when the celebrity transcends into the world of reality. Am I the reality or am I simply just trying to escape my world into the world of the celebrity? It's something that I do question from time to time. Why do I need to build this collection and at what stage is my collection finished? Think about it, there is always going to be another celebrity to meet and it will go on and on.

After twenty years of having my photo taken with celebrities I feel that my collection, which I consider to be my body of work, is ready for you to see. Is it a work of art I hear you say? Is there an art to getting your photo next to someone that is famous?

Let me ask you this, is there an art to playing tennis where you simply hit a ball over a net or is there an art to golf where you hit a ball into a hole then do it all over again for a further seventeen holes. Like any athlete, I do my homework on how to go about meeting a celebrity, just as a coach would do for his or her team. I place myself in a position where I know that I am going to encounter a meeting with a celebrity. Like a soccer coach will train his players on where they should stand to give them the best advantage to win the game, by me waiting at hotels, airports or celebrity 'hangouts' I am simply putting myself in the best position to meet a celebrity.

This book represents a collection of photographs which uniquely documents my life through photos from 1989 until 2007. My hair has come and gone. My baby face has turned into that of an adult and my clothes of mostly surfing apparel have now progressed into jeans and shirts.

Life as we all know is being documented every day, from camera phones, digital cameras, video cameras and security cameras. We as human beings are being documented. I, in what I do am no different from you, though the people that I have documented have been labelled as celebrities. The world of the celebrity is very different from our day to day life, its something that's fascinated me for most of my adult life.

So the next time you're in a hotel room and you open the side drawer next to your bed, don't be surprised to find that the Bible has been replaced with a celebrity gossip magazine. But STOP! Before you panic, there's no need to. You can breath a sigh of relief—the magazine is this week's edition. You haven't missed a thing!

Richard Simpkin
March 2007

So you want to meet a celebrity...

Well, it's 10am and you've just got to the hotel where a certain celebrity you want to meet is staying. Five hours pass and you have seen no sign of the celebrity. You have been getting very bad looks from the hotel staff, you're hungry, you're thirsty and you are busting to go to the toilet. After a few more hours you're getting cold and seriously bored.

You're about to call it a day when suddenly four security guards come out of the hotel; they come out the front where you are waiting, have a look around, assess the situation then walk back into the hotel where they gather with two public relations girls. The girls notice that you are standing outside obviously waiting for their prized star, they say a few words to the security then check their clipboards to make sure everything is going to plan. A moment passes and two of the security guards come out the front of the hotel and walk directly over to you: 'Excuse me, sir, can I help you'?

You reply in your most polite voice, 'No, I'm okay thank you.'

They then ask, 'Can I ask who you are waiting for?'

You say either:

1. You are waiting for the celebrity they are looking after to see if you can get your photo taken with them; or

2. You tell them that you aren't waiting for anyone in particular and you are simply waiting outside the hotel enjoying the beautiful day.

Either answer doesn't really change the situation because it's all just a game—it's you versus them and in theory you should be defeated through sheer manpower. But determination somehow takes control of you and you stand your ground. After a few more words are exchanged the security guards walk back into the hotel and have a mini meeting about what steps they're going to take so you don't get a chance to ask the celebrity for a photo or an autograph.

A moment passes and the two security guards come back out and walk over to you. They inform you that you are on private property and that they are going to call the police. You in turn inform them that you are standing on a public footpath and you ask them to call the police, knowing that it will be embarrassing if the police do come only to find one or two people standing on the public footpath.

Twenty more minutes pass and the two hired cars that have been sitting out the front of the hotel start their engines. You say to yourself 'here we go', your heart is pumping a million miles an hour and you are so nervous that you would rather be back at school sitting a major final year exam than waiting outside the hotel.

Another minute passes and three or four doormen come out the front of the hotel to add extra manpower to the beefed-up security team. The hotel manager appears and looks directly at you, thinking his stare will be enough to send you running home scared. It doesn't.

You can feel the nervous energy in the air. Now you're up against security guys, three or four doorman, two public relations girls and two limousine drivers/security guards. Then the moment arrives.

You see the celebrity walking through the hotel lobby with their *own* security team. The adrenaline kicks in; you take a step towards the front of the hotel and the hotel security guards very quickly walk towards you, yelling at the top of their voices to 'get back, get back'. The hotel staff panic; thinking that they need to prove their own importance. They follow in the security team's footsteps waving their hands in the air, yelling at you and trying to block access to the celebrity.

You pay no attention to any of them and wait for the split second the celebrity walks out the front of the hotel doors. You yell out: 'Mr or Miss [Celebrity], may I have my photo taken with you?' Your friend holds up a poster and asks if he or she will sign it for him, the celebrity gives you a smile and asks you to come on over to them as they are happy to sign and pose for a photo.

You go to walk over to the celebrity but one of the security team has lost control and grabs your shirt and aggressively pushes you away from the hotel. You try to explain that the celebrity has agreed to meet you and you hear the celebrity yell out that it's okay for us to come over to meet him or her.

Security, public relations girls, doormen and limousine drivers all look at you in disbelief as you casually walk over to the celebrity. Your friend gets his poster signed, then you get your photo taken with the celebrity, you then very politely thank the celebrity for their time and wish them good luck in whatever they have come out to promote.

Within ten seconds it's all over. The celebrity gets in the car while the hotel manager tells you to get off the hotel's property, which you are obviously doing anyway as you've got what you wanted. The look on everyone's face is priceless—no-one can believe that somehow you got through all of those people to get to the celebrity.

All that waiting is quickly forgotten; the battle was won and you feel the highest high.

You get the film developed and hope and pray that the photo turns out. If it does you put it in your album, close the album, then take a look at your calendar to see which celebrity is next in town.

Welcome to my world.

INXS 1989

In late 1989 I was told by a friend at school that INXS were rehearsing for their new album at the Sydney Opera House. One day after school I went down to the Opera House with my friend to see if I could meet them. After a few minutes of walking around we found the band in the back of a truck doing a photo shoot. My friend and I waited for them to have a break and when they did we simply walked up to them and asked for a group photo and they happily obliged.

Sammy Davis Jr 1989

In 1989 entertainers Frank Sinatra, Liza Minnelli and Sammy Davis Jr toured Australia for a show called *The Ultimate Event*. I spent a few days waiting for the three legends to return to their hotel but I wasn't able to meet any of them. I was just fifteen and these were the very first international acts I had ever tried to meet. Maybe I aimed too high—think about it: Sinatra, Minnelli and Sammy Davis Jr!

A few months later Sammy came back out to Sydney to do some charity events. I heard that he was going to be on a local television show that was to be shot live on location in the city of Sydney. I went down to the location and found myself right at the back of about 300 well-wishers of Sammy's. Just as he was about to leave the television show I asked him if I could have my photo with him. Sammy happily gave me the photo. Little did I know that this was to be the start of it all.

Billy Joel and Christie Brinkley 1990

These two photos were taken in 1990 when musician Billy Joel and model Christie Brinkley were still married. Just as the photo of Billy and me was taken a driver who didn't like the idea of me meeting celebrities yelled out for the photo not to be taken. I think the look on my face shows that I was slightly scared. A moment later Christie got out of her car and posed for this photo— the driver was still yelling at me but I learnt to ignore him, and so did Billy and Christie.

Bobby Brown 1990

When musician Bobby Brown came to Sydney in 1990 he was a huge star. Every day at his hotel there were about 50 screaming girls waiting to see him. When he did come in and out of the hotel his security team would surround him and it was nearly impossible to get anywhere near him.

I had been at the hotel for about three days waiting for the moment when I could ask for my photo with him. On the last night of his Sydney shows I was the only fan waiting for him to leave because all of the other fans had gone to his concert. When Bobby came out to leave for the show I asked him if I could have a photo with him.

He nodded to his security that it was okay for me to walk on over to him. I handed my camera to one of his minders, who took the photo. I couldn't believe that I had finally got a photo with him, but when I got the photo developed I was horrified to see that he had purposely put the video camera in front of his face so that I didn't get the photo—what a great guy! Not. I wonder whatever happened to Bobby Brown. Ha ha!

Cher 1990

I had waited to meet singer/actor Cher for a few days at her hotel but every day when she left and came back to the hotel she went in and out of the car park so there was no way of meeting her. One night after one of her shows she came back to the hotel and was about to drive straight into the hotel's car park.

I was waiting for her with one other fan, and just as the car was about to enter the car park it stopped and a hand from the back seat waved us over, Cher was sitting in the limo in full concert gear; she signed a few items for both of us and I snapped this photo of her just as she was about to drive off.

In 2005 when Cher came back to Sydney for her farewell tour I waited again for her as I was never able to get a photo with her—once again she was using the hotel's car park to get in and out, but this time I had no luck. Four nights in a row she drove into the car park without stopping.

Elton John 1990

I met singer/songwriter Elton John at the Sebel Townhouse Hotel when he was on tour in 1990. During the day he was nice and accessible, posing for photos and signing autographs for a few of his fans who were waiting at the hotel. At night, however, as he was leaving and coming back from his concert he was the complete opposite. We were told by his people that Elton was not to be approached at night.

One night a girl came down to the hotel and wanted to get Elton's autograph. I told her that he wouldn't stop when he was leaving or coming back from the show. She didn't care and waited out the front of the hotel for Elton to leave for his concert. Just before he was to leave the hotel the doorman, Hans, got out the hotel's hose and turned it full blast on the girl. Let's just say that she didn't get the autograph.

This was a common thing for Hans the doorman to do. Over the years he would always tell us fans that if we went across the road to try to meet anyone famous he would get out the hotel's hose and wet us with it. After a few drenchings I brought down some eggs to the hotel, and one day when Hans was about to get out the hose I produced the eggs. It was a bit of a Mexican stand-off but Hans put the hose away. I guess he thought that it wouldn't be a good look for him to be looking and smelling like an egg as the hotel's VIPs passed by.

Eric Clapton 1990

I met musician Eric in 1990 when he was on tour in Australia. When Eric came off his Sydney flight I was the only one waiting for him at the airport. As soon as he got out of the terminal he lit up a cigarette and mingled with his entourage, and after his smoke he came over to me and gave me a photo.

On one particular night after his concert, I was waiting for him to arrive at his hotel because a friend of mine wanted to get something signed. As we were waiting we saw a guy parking his Harley Davidson out the front of the hotel. After a moment or two I noticed that it was Craig Johnston, an Australian soccer star. I asked Craig what he was up to, and he replied that he was a fan of Eric's and was waiting to see him just like we were.

After some time Eric came back to the hotel, signed my friend's programme and noticed Craig waiting out the front of the hotel. Eric instantly recognised Craig and invited him into the hotel's bar for a few drinks. It's strange to think that celebrities wait for other celebrities outside hotels and venues, etc. It just goes to show that anyone can be a fan.

Joe Montana 1990

In 1990 my friend, who was a huge San Francisco 49ers fan, rang me and told me that his hero, former gridiron player Joe Montana, the quarterback for the 49ers, was in town to shoot a commercial. In those days you could simply ring the hotels and ask if a celebrity was staying there, and after ringing I found out where the gridiron legend was staying.

We were told by my friend's dad that we would not get Montana because he had read that he only signed autographs for money. This was something we had never heard of in Australia in 1990. We collected a few things to get signed and went down to the hotel. Lucky for us we only had to wait about an hour before Montana left the hotel. He signed a few autographs and posed for some photos, slightly amused that these two kids were making such a fuss over him when he was virtually unknown in Australia at that time.

Kylie Minogue 1990

This photo of songbird Kylie and me was taken when she was dating Michael Hutchence. Kylie used to visit Michael at Rhinoceros Recording Studios while he and the rest of INXS were recording their album *X*. I used to wait in the foyer of the recording studios for INXS.

I have to say that of all of the celebrities I have been lucky enough to meet, Kylie is one of the nicest. She always has time for her fans. I've never seen her turn down a request for a photo or an autograph, and let me tell you there are some pretty crazy Kylie fans. Speaking of crazy, look at Kylie's hair and clothes.

MC Hammer 1990

In 1990 musician MC Hammer was one of the biggest music stars in the world, second only to Michael Jackson. When he toured Sydney in 1990 I was lucky enough to meet him on a few occasions.

There were a lot of fans searching for him at different hotels around town but I got the correct hotel the day he arrived thanks to a tip-off from the doorman at this hotel. MC Hammer was his own biggest fan—as you can see he is wearing his own concert T-shirt. When he came out of the hotel on this particular day, he had a huge posse with him and two of them had huge ghetto blasters playing his music.

After he posed for a few photos for me he got in the limousine undid all the windows, undid the sunroof on the limo and played his music full blast from his limo and the three cars that followed. I have to say though that he was extremely nice to me and many other fans and always posed for photos and signed everyone's autographs.

The following year he put out a song called 'Too Legit to Quit', with a video clip that cost millions of dollars and quotes from him saying that he was going to be bigger than Michael Jackson. Sadly within a few months MC Hammer was out of the spotlight and Michael Jackson held onto his reign as King of Pop. Well, for a few more years anyway.

Melissa Etheridge 1990

When musician Melissa came to Sydney in 1990 for some shows she wasn't a huge star like she is now. I knew this because she stayed in a hotel called 17. Celebrities stayed at the Sebel Townhouse Hotel, lesser known celebrities stayed at 17.

The morning that I met Melissa she came out and asked me where she could find a chemist so that she could buy some tampons. Now I was a 16-year-old kid and I almost died of embarrassment. Lucky for me the moment didn't last too long; there was a chemist a few metres down the road.

Milli Vanilli 1990

Pop group Milli Vanilli (Fab Morvan and Rob Pilatus) were a duo from Germany that won a Grammy in 1990 for Best New Artist.

Milli Vanilli had three number one hits in the US all from the one album: 'Girl I'm Gonna Miss You', 'Baby Don't Forget My Number' and 'Blame It On The Rain'.

In 1990 when Rob and Fab were in Sydney on a promotional trip I went down to the Sebel Townhouse. There were about six girls waiting for the boys to leave the hotel. When they did I quickly went up to them and got a photo in between them. At the time this was a prized photo for me. Unfortunately some months later it was discovered that they did not sing on their album and their Grammy was taken away from them. In 1998 Rob Pilatus died of a drug overdose and the pop group that was once one of the biggest acts in the world is now just a faded memory.

It's funny now to think about it, but in 1990 when they were in town I missed a school camp just so I could meet them. When my friends came back from camp this photo was the talk of the school (for about a day—or maybe two).

Nelson Mandela 1990

The first country that humanitarian/world leader Nelson Mandela visited after his release from jail was Australia. Mandela's movements after being released from jail were a huge story for the world's media. I waited at his hotel for him to arrive with a few other well-wishers. He arrived at his Sydney hotel with full police protection. He was quickly escorted into the hotel and out of the public eye.

I was only 16 at the time but I knew that this would be a hugely important photo for my collection. I looked in the newspaper and found Mandela's public appearances. After going to a few of his scheduled appearances and actually walking next to him a few times, I was turned down by Mandela for a photo with him. Another guy who also really wanted to meet him kept popping up at his appearances to try to get Mandela's autograph, but Mandela refused his requests.

After a few days the autograph guy said to me that he was giving up, as Mandela didn't want to be 'fan' friendly. I knew that I had one more chance and it was all or nothing. Mandela was due to give a speech at the Hilton Hotel. I arrived about an hour before his scheduled speech. Out the front of the hotel were about 20 media—mostly photographers and about 20 well-wishers. The lobby of the Hilton was filled with security and police.

I waited calmly inside the hotel's foyer with my mum. I knew when Mandela had arrived because I could hear all of the fuss outside the hotel. I quickly thought of a plan: I told my mum that I would simply walk straight up to Mandela when he entered the hotel foyer, and once I got next to him she was to take the photo. Mandela arrived in the foyer surrounded by about 10 security with a further 15 police.

I simply walked straight up to Mandela and asked him for a photo. I can tell you I caught the security and the police completely off guard. Mandela simply looked at me in disbelief and laughed, while my mum quickly snapped the photo. I had a photo with Nelson Mandela!

I can tell you that if I tried this trick today I would probably get arrested. Being a 16-year-old kid and looking about 14 I could get away with almost anything.

Pelé 1990

In 1990 soccer star Pelé, who is regarded as the greatest soccer player to have ever played the game, visited Sydney. I had read that he was going to be at the Sydney Football Stadium to watch a game. After the game, about 50 people gathered around Pelé's car. When he came out to the car everyone rushed at him. He didn't have any security so he quickly got into his car, but as soon as he was in his car he opened the window and signed autographs for all of the fans. I realised that I couldn't get a photo with him then and there, so I left the stadium before him and went to his hotel where I was the only one waiting for him. I got a few photos of him and with him.

Shirley MacLaine 1990

As a child I used to love watching the old Hollywood movies, so even as a kid I thought that the legends were far more important to meet than the current celebrities. Actor Shirley MacLaine is a Hollywood legend. In 1958 she was nominated for an Academy Award for *Some Came Running*, and received a second Academy Award nomination for *The Apartment* (1960). Three years later, she received a third nomination for *Irma la Douce* (1963).

In 1975 Shirley made a documentary on China called *The Other Half of the Sky: A China Memoir* for which she received an Oscar nomination for Best Documentary. In 1977 she got her fourth Best Actor Oscar nomination for *The Turning Point*. Shirley finally took home the Oscar for Best Actor in 1983 for *Terms of Endearment*.

I met Shirley outside her Sydney hotel in 1990 when she was in Sydney to perform some shows. She was very nice and was happy to pose for some photos for me and sign some autographs. It's funny to look at this photo now and see how young I was when I first started my photo collection.

Steve Tyler 1990

I first met Aerosmith musician Steve Tyler and the rest of Aerosmith when they were in Sydney to perform for their world tour promoting the album *Pump*.

The first time that I met Steve was by pure luck. Aerosmith arrived in Sydney a few days before their shows and they were having a holiday with their families. I just happened to be trying to find out where Australian Opera singer Dame Joan Sutherland was staying and noticed a few fans waiting outside the Sebel Townhouse.

I quickly put aside my Joan Sutherland mission and ran up to the local shop where I bought a magazine. At the time Aerosmith were huge and they were on the covers of most of the music magazines. I rushed back down to the hotel and after a few days got all of their autographs and photos.

The strange thing was that when they started their Australian tour and came back to Sydney they changed hotels. This photo was taken of Steve one night as he was waiting for his wife to come down to the lobby so they could get some dinner. Steve noticed me and a few other fans waiting for him so he came over to us, signed some autographs and posed for some photos. He looks just like any other tourist. Just check out his pants!

In 2004 I met Steve again outside a restaurant in Beverly Hills. Once again I got my photo taken with him. Remarkably Steve looks younger in my 2004 photo than he did in 1990. Some people in showbiz just seem to age better than the rest of us, don't they?

Tom Jones 1990

I met singer Tom Jones in Sydney when he was here to do some concerts for his 1990 Australian tour. This photo was taken at his press conference, which he was doing to promote his shows.

In 1990 there was no such thing as having your name on a media list for any press conference. I simply used to ring up a few photographers and ask them what was coming up over the next couple of days. If there was a press conference I simply used to walk in wearing my surf T-shirt and shorts and take photos with my $90 camera. After the press conference I used to walk up to the celebrity and have my photo taken with them and if they had any promo photos I had them signed.

Up until about 1998 getting into a press conference almost guaranteed you a meeting with that particular celebrity. Today there are almost more security guards at the press conference than there are press. Today it's almost impossible to meet the celebrity after the press conference.

Tommy Lee 1990

Before Tommy Lee was famous for being married to and divorced from Pamela Anderson and having his own reality television show, he was simply the drummer of the band Mötley Crüe. When Mötley Crüe toured Australia in 1990 for their Dr Feelgood world tour they were one of the biggest bands in the world. I was sixteen at the time and was a huge fan. I guessed by their tour dates what day they were going to be in Sydney.

That day I went down to the Sebel Townhouse and waited with about 60 or so other Mötley fans. After waiting most of the day my friend and I went up to Kings Cross (Sydney's red light district) to get some food. While we were up at the shops four stretched limousines drove through Kings Cross; we both knew that it was the four members of the band. We ran as fast as we could and were lucky to get to the hotel just before they arrived. When the four limousines arrived out the front of the hotel, all of the fans started screaming and running towards them. The band had no choice but to quickly run into the hotel.

As the days passed I met each member of the band. One day in particular stands out. It was about day three of the band's stay in Sydney and a kid aged about 15 had been waiting to meet his idol Tommy Lee. Tommy came out of the hotel and this kid sees him and just runs across the road towards Tommy. Unfortunately there was a car driving past the hotel; the car hit the kid, the kid bounced off the front of the car slammed onto the ground got up and kept running towards Tommy!

Everyone was in total shock. Tommy's security guard took Tommy back into the hotel, and Tommy asked his security to go and bring the kid over to him. The kid came out of the hotel about an hour later with a pair of Tommy Lee's drum sticks, a few sets of Mötley Crüe autographs and a smile that said it all. He was later taken to hospital where he was told that he had broken a few ribs. Now that's dedication to your favourite heavy metal band.

Whoopi Goldberg 1990

In 1990 actor Whoopi toured Australia with one of her stand-up shows. On her first Sydney show I waited with a friend for Whoopi to arrive at the theatre where she was to perform her show. As we were waiting a homeless guy came up to us and asked what we were doing. We told him that we were just hanging around; we didn't want to tell him that we were waiting for Whoopi Goldberg—the less people that are waiting for a celebrity the better chance you have of getting them.

But for some reason the guy didn't want to leave us alone. He sat next to us and asked us for money and cigarettes. Eventually Whoopi arrived at the theatre. She was very friendly and posed for some photos and signed some autographs; the guy didn't know who she was nor did he care but he did ask her for some money and cigarettes. Whoopi was slightly embarrassed but handled the situation well. She didn't have any money on her and didn't smoke and after this rejection the guy finally gave up and left. Strangely enough Whoopi couldn't get into the theatre and stayed out the back of the venue with us until someone arrived and realised that it was Whoopi Goldberg waiting outside her own gig. What a strange day.

Audrey Hepburn 1991

This priceless photo of actor Audrey Hepburn and I really sums it up why I have my photo
taken with celebrities. Even though I'm not a huge fan of Audrey's movies the photo that
I have with her is in my top five out of almost 1000 celebrities. I met Audrey in Sydney when she
was here as an ambassador for UNICEF. I rang UNICEF one morning and told them that I wanted to meet Audrey
Hepburn. The lady that I spoke to told me what hotel she was staying at but added that I better get to the hotel very soon as she
was about to check out and leave the country (how times have changed!).

I rushed down to her hotel and met her as she was leaving. I had a photo from the movie *Sabrina*, which Audrey starred in
with William Holden and Humphrey Bogart. She was kind enough to sign the photo and told me that I couldn't get the other
two as they had passed away. I was just happy to have Audrey sign it. After she signed a few items for me I asked her if I could
have my photo taken with her. She agreed to my request but added that she was in a bit of a rush. Gracious as ever, she posed
for the photo and got into her waiting limousine.

I still have to pinch myself sometimes when I look at this photo; Audrey Hepburn is one of the most famous people in the
world and there I am standing next to her—surreal.

Bob Geldof 1991

It's the 1991 ARIAs (Australian Record Industry Awards), Australia's equivalent to the Grammys, in Sydney. I turn up to the event in tracksuit pants, a football jersey, sneakers and my $90 camera. I'm standing out the front of the awards taking photos of the celebrities as they are walking in, when a lady comes up to me and asks, 'Are you a photographer?' to which I replied, 'Yes'.

'Well then what are you doing outside?' she asks. She then tells me to follow her, and the next thing you know I'm inside the awards ceremony right up the front of the stage taking photos of Mick Fleetwood and activist/musician Bob Geldof. As the night continues the lady who took me inside somehow thinks that I'm the head photographer so she asks me to tell the other photographers what the correct procedures are for the night. Now remember I'm a kid, wearing clothes that make me look like I've been at the gym and I've got a $90 camera around my neck! So being a good kid I follow orders and relay messages to the other photographers on what was expected of them throughout the night. Let's just say that everyone was very confused including me.

As the night continued I noticed that Bob Geldof was sitting behind a curtain that was attached to the side of the stage rehearsing his lines before he was to go on stage to present the night's major award. I walked behind the curtain and took this photo of Bob. He was so into reading his lines that he didn't even notice that I had taken the photo. A bizarre night all round.

Dannii Minogue 1991

In the early 1990s I was a huge Dannii fan. Every time she was in Sydney I used to go and wait for her at the Sebel Townhouse Hotel. As the years passed singer Dannii started to remember me and would always greet me with a smile and a hug. Though she didn't reach the same level of fame as her sister Kylie, Dannii became hugely successful in the UK, where like her sister she has become a gay icon.

I took this photo of Dannii in 1991 when she was in Sydney to promote one of her singles. On this particular night there were about ten fans waiting for her at the hotel. Dannii came outside, sat on the steps of the hotel and signed autographs for all of us, she posed for photos and chatted to us for over half an hour. She's always been really great to her fans.

Elvis Costello 1991

Has Elvis left the building, or is he just hiding underneath all of that hair? I always say to people that there's something about a celebrity that makes them stand out. I mean, it's usually their five bodyguards or their entourage, but they really do somehow stand out. Musician Elvis Costello was on tour in Australia and I was waiting for him at the Sebel Townhouse Hotel. I didn't know that he had grown his hair and beard, but as soon as this guy walked out the front of the hotel I knew it had to be Elvis Costello. Was he in disguise when he left the building? Who knows but I can tell you that he was a really nice guy. I bumped into him again in 2003 while I was in LA and he was just as cool. It's great to see that he has stayed the same. Well, except for the long hair and beard.

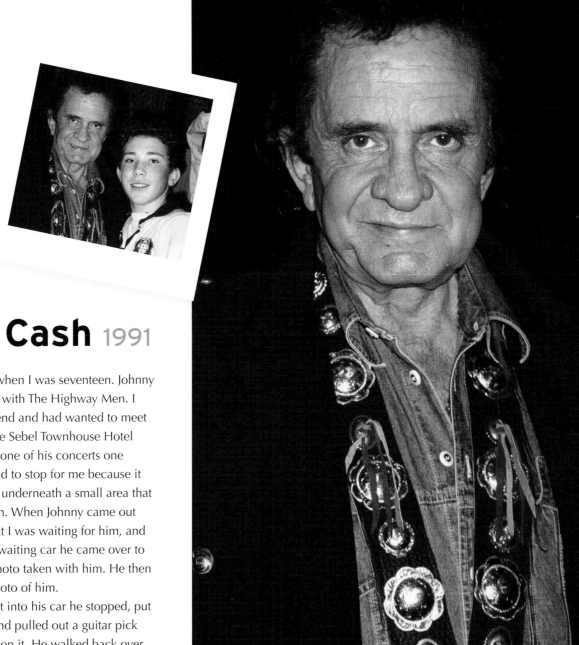

Johnny Cash 1991

I took this photo in 1991 when I was seventeen. Johnny was in Sydney performing with The Highway Men. I knew that Cash was a legend and had wanted to meet him. I waited for him at the Sebel Townhouse Hotel and met him as he left for one of his concerts one night. Johnny was very kind to stop for me because it was raining. I was waiting underneath a small area that was sheltered from the rain. When Johnny came out of the hotel he noticed that I was waiting for him, and instead of getting into his waiting car he came over to me and let me have my photo taken with him. He then posed so I could take a photo of him.

As he was leaving to get into his car he stopped, put his hand into his pocket and pulled out a guitar pick that had his name printed on it. He walked back over to me and gave me the guitar pick. Truly a man of the people.

Meat Loaf and Gunnar Nelson 1991

In 1991 Pepsi gathered a whole bunch of celebrities and flew them to Australia to enjoy days and days of activities such as golf, tennis, softball and cocktail parties. Wouldn't it be nice to be a celebrity? On this particular day the celebrities, including Olivia Newton-John, Leslie Nielsen, Ray Parker Jr, Vince Neil (Mötley Crüe), singers Meat Loaf and Matthew and Gunnar Nelson, were all taken to some tennis courts for a day of tennis, drinks and a laugh with the Tooheys models.

In this photo singer Gunnar Nelson, the son of former rocker Ricky Nelson, and Meat Loaf are posing with the Tooheys models. It was a really great couple of days for the celebs and the fans.

Morrissey 1991

In 1991 musician Morrissey arrived in Sydney for his Australian tour. The first day he arrived I went down to the Sebel Townhouse Hotel to try to meet him with about five other fans.

He came out of the hotel just after lunch, signed a few autographs and didn't really say too much. He seemed to be very shy and kept to himself. In fact his autograph is a lot different to other stars' autographs, as he simply prints the word *MORRISSEY*.

After meeting with me and the other fans he went back into the hotel and the next day it was in the paper that he had cancelled his Australian tour. That morning, about fifteen Morrissey fans rushed down to the hotel to try to meet him but he had checked out of the hotel that morning and sadly for the Morrissey fans in Australia he hasn't returned. I was lucky to have snapped this photo.

The Queen and Prince Phillip 1991

The Queen was in Sydney with Prince Phillip in 1991. I took this photo as she was leaving Royal Randwick Race Course where they had spent the day at the races. A number of admirers were waiting to see the royal couple. As they drove down the street and away from the majority of the crowd I took this single photo. It's one of my favourite photos, as even though they were out in full view of the public, it's almost like a private moment between them. When I look at this photo I always wonder what the Queen is thinking.

Wendy and Nick
from TransVision Vamp

Wendy James 1991

The first girl I ever had a crush on was Wendy James, a musician and member of TransVision Vamp.
To me, a sixteen-year-old in 1989, Wendy James was the hottest girl on the planet.

Fast forward two years to 1991 when I was eighteen and Wendy's band TransVision Vamp were on their second tour of Australia. If Wendy was somewhere in Sydney then chances were I was there too! I met her at the airport where I had this photo taken with her. I met her at the hotel, sound check, back at the hotel again and then for the last time at the international airport when she was leaving—oops I mean when the band were leaving!

One night after their concert I was waiting with about six other fans for her to arrive back at the hotel. When Wendy arrived she invited all of us into the hotel's bar for a night of drinks. I could hardly believe my luck. As I was walking up the stairs to enter the hotel, the hotel's manager came out and stopped me from entering the hotel; he had a real grudge against me because I was always waiting for celebs outside his hotel. Wendy walked into the hotel with the other fans and headed straight for the bar. I yelled out to her but she didn't hear me and what could have been the best night of my life was all over within seconds.

Anthony Kiedis 1992

These two photos of Red Hot Chili Peppers singer Anthony Kiedis may be the only
photos from the Red Hot Chili Peppers 1992 Australian tour. The Peppers were in Sydney to
perform some concerts. I went down to their hotel to wait for them and John Cougar Mellencamp who was also in
town for some shows. One night I was getting Mellencamp's autograph when the tour manger walked into the hotel looking very
upset. Mellencamp asked the tour manager what was wrong, and he told Mellencamp that the guitarist from the Chili Peppers
had just quit the band and that rehearsals with a new guitarist weren't working.

The three remaining members from the Chili Peppers were really cool. These two photos show a very young and relaxed
Anthony. His arms are open because he was chasing one of his entourage's kids around the hotel. A few months after these
photos were taken the Red Hot Chili Peppers were one of the biggest bands in the world.

Elle Macpherson 1992

I took this photo of supermodel Elle in 1992 when she was at 2DAY FM radio station. It was a few years before paparazzi had taken off in Sydney. Before 1993 I used to just hang out at hotels, airports, radio and television stations and take happy snaps of the stars. After 1993 it all changed. Today if Elle went to a radio station there would be photographers trying to get their exclusive photo and security guards and PR people trying to protect their 'prized star'.

Elle is usually pretty good when it comes to autographs and photos but as I found out in about 1997 she won't sign any nude photos of herself. In about 1997 I was at the airport waiting for her to arrive, and when she did I asked her to sign a beautiful and tasteful photo of herself nude, taken by world renowned photographer Patrick Demarchelier. She grabbed the pen from me and threw it on the ground, turned around and shouted: 'I don't sign naked photos of myself, I have a child you know.'

I just stood there in shock; the photo was such a beautiful, artistic black and white photo that she had obviously posed for—it wasn't a paparazzi photo of her at the beach; even her PR girl apologised to me. I'm guessing it was a bad day at the office for 'The Body'. If you don't like nude photos of yourself, then don't pose for them.

Flavor Flav 1992

In the mid 1980s to the early 1990s Public Enemy were one of the biggest rap bands in the world. They were definitely one of the most influential rap bands of their time. I was a huge fan of their music. In 1992 Public Enemy toured Australia and musician Flavor Flav, who you could say was the Jerry Lewis of the band, used to go everywhere with a huge clock around his neck, and I mean everywhere—shopping centres, airports, hotels, even the beach.

One day my mum was driving my friend and me to the hotel to meet Public Enemy, when out of the corner of my eye I saw Flavor Flav playing basketball with his two huge bodyguards and his clock around his neck! My mum stopped the car and I got out and walked over to the courts. Flav called me over and asked what I was up to, I told him that I was on my way to his hotel to try to meet him. He then asked if he could get a lift back to his hotel, and of course I said yes. You should have seen mum's face when I walked up from the basketball courts with Flavor Flav, his two bodyguards, my friend and me!

We then all climbed into mum's small car. When we got to the hotel Flav invited me, my mum and my friend into the hotel for some lunch. When we got out of the car, another friend of mine who I was supposed to meet at the hotel was waiting for Flav to turn up; he does—but with me and my mum. My friend gets Flav's autograph and then asked for another. Flav tells him that he is with friends and can he sign his stuff after lunch—the look on my friend's face was priceless. During lunch the two bodyguards stood at the front of the restaurant so nobody could interrupt us. Lunch lasted for about an hour and I got to feel what it was like to be a celebrity for all of that hour. What a day!

Ice T 1992

In 1992 actor/musician Ice T toured Australia with his band Bodycount. Though he was known then as a rapper, his band Bodycount was a heavy metal band that had a controversial song on their CD called 'Cop Killer'. There was so much controversy at the time of the album's release that the CD was pulled from the shelves and re-released with the song removed.

Ice T found a whole new wave of fans including me. I took this photo of Ice as he was leaving for one of his shows. Fast forward ten years and Ice T has now another new wave of fans with his role in television's top rating crime show *Law and Order* in which, ironically, he plays a cop!

Nirvana 1992

It's January 1992 and grunge band Nirvana are fast becoming one of the most talked about bands in
the world. They have a song out called 'Smells Like Teen Spirit', which completely blows everyone's mind away. It was
the beginning of grunge. Nirvana, Pearl Jam and Soundgarden were at the top of the charts with their new sound. Nirvana was
in Sydney to perform at the very first Big Day Out, a music festival that tours Australia and New Zealand every summer.

The day that I was going to meet the band I rang a bunch of my friends and asked them if they wanted to come and meet
Nirvana with me. Half of my friends said 'Who'? The other half couldn't care less. One friend had nothing else to do so she
came along. After a few hours of waiting, Kurt Cobain walked out of the small boutique hotel and walked over to us. He signed
a few items for me and posed for a photo. He didn't mutter a word, and although my friend suggested that I have my photo
taken with him, I looked at the bleeding scabs on his face and politely said that I didn't want a photo with him.

He went for a walk up to Kings Cross, Sydney's red light district, but was only up there for about fifteen minutes. An hour
later Kurt and Courtney Love came out of the hotel and got into a fight, which ended with Courtney throwing Kurt onto their
rented van—I wish I had those photos. A few hours later Chris and Dave Grohl, who is now the front man for the Foo Fighters,
came back to the hotel. They signed my stuff and posed for this photo. They told me and my friend that they had just had a crash
in their rented van and they were both laughing about it.

Robert Smith 1992

In 1992 The Cure toured Australia and I found out that they were staying at the Ritz Carlton Hotel in Double Bay, Sydney's answer to Beverly Hills. When band member Robert Smith arrived after the concert I got out of the car and went to walk over to him, when all of a sudden four security guards came from out of nowhere and blocked my access to him. I called out to him and he called me over. He signed some things for me and posed for a few photos. I was surprised by how nice he was. He went into the hotel and settled in to wait for the other band members to arrive.

The hotel's security started to panic, and told me that The Cure members were the first celebrities that had stayed at the hotel and they didn't want pesky fans waiting outside their prestigious hotel. They warned me that if I continued waiting they would take me out the back and belt the crap out of me! I tried to explain to them that I was the only one who knew where the band were staying and they didn't have to worry about one fan waiting for the band. The security warned me again to leave or else. I then told them that if they didn't leave me alone I would tell every Cure fan that I knew where the band was staying and that they would have a bunch of dedicated Robert Smith lookalikes waiting outside their prestigious hotel in no time.

I left the hotel that night without meeting the other members—but I had a plan. The following night I went to the back of the concert door and found about 30 Cure fans and told them where the band was staying. They all rushed to the hotel and waited out the front for the band to arrive. The security guys ran outside and panicked, they got out their walkie talkies called for extra security and gave me fantastic death stares. When Robert Smith arrived back at the hotel the security surrounded him and tried to rush him in. To his credit he asked the security to back off, walked over to the fans and signed autographs and posed for photos for every fan, even allowing the female fans to give him kisses—we couldn't have asked for anything more. I've always had trouble with security, hardly ever with the celebrity. On this occasion it was a win for me and the other Cure fans.

Tori Amos 1992

Before 1992 I had never heard of Tori Amos, but in mid 1992 I heard a song called 'Crucify.' I had never heard a song like it. I rushed out and bought the album *Silent All These Years* and was completely blown away by Tori's voice, lyrics and the way she sang and composed her songs. A few weeks after I bought the album Tori came to Sydney on a promo visit.

I was the only fan waiting for her at the hotel for the few days that she was in town. She was very cute and friendly and was a little embarrassed that I was such a fan of hers. The following year Tori toured Australia and everywhere she went a bunch of fans followed her.

Today in 2007 Tori Amos has a huge underground fan base in Australia and when she comes back to perform some shows, 50 or so fans wait for her wherever she goes. I'm just glad I was one of the first to meet her on her first visit to Australia in 1992.

Brooke Shields 1993

In 1993 actor Brooke Shields came to Sydney to film the movie *The Seventh Floor*. While she was in Sydney I found out that she was going to be a special guest at a trendy warehouse party. Luckily for me I was able to obtain a ticket to the same party. As soon as I walked in I saw Brooke having a dance, she had no bodyguards and as I found out no ego. I had a chat with her during the night and even had a dance with her for a few songs.

Sadly for me no cameras were allowed at the party; however, I managed to take this photo of Brooke as she was arriving at a play at the Seymour Centre in Sydney. When she arrived she couldn't find the entrance, though eventually she did!

Helena Christensen 1993

In 1993, model Helena Christensen was the most stunning female I had ever met in my entire life. I know that's a big quote, but I can honestly say that she simply had 'that something' that I had never seen before, an exotic and natural beauty. At the time she was Michael Hutchence's girlfriend. I was pretty lucky in those days to have been able to spend a bit of time with Helena, due to her relationship with Michael.

Helena used to hang outside with me in the foyer of the studio where INXS used to record their albums for hours and hours and tell me about Europe and her life as a model. I took this photo of Helena while she was waiting for Michael to arrive at Sydney Airport. INXS were touring around Australia and Helena had some modelling to do in Sydney. While we were waiting for Michael to arrive I asked her if I could take a photo of her. Just as I was about to take the photo she told me to wait a moment, she then undid the top two buttons on her shirt and opened it up a little bit, then gave me the AOK to take the photo. After a few seconds of daydreaming I snapped back into reality and took the photo. Thank you God for Helena Christensen. Amen.

Iggy Pop 1993

Musician Iggy Pop is as cool as they come. I took this photo of him at Sydney Airport when he arrived to do some concerts. I was the only fan at the airport to greet him. He was really nice and down to earth and signed a few records for me. As I was about to take this photo Iggy asked me to wait a minute, took off his reading glasses and posed in true Iggy style.

I met him again in 2006 when he was in town for some shows, and he was just as relaxed and friendly. There were six other fans waiting for him. He got off the plane with an injured foot, saw us waiting for him and asked us (!) if we would sit down with him while he signed everyone's autographs and posed for photos. Thirteen years on and he was still just as cool.

Jon Bon Jovi
and
Ritchie Sambora 1993

Now to be a true rock star you need a few things like long hair, sunglasses, jewellery around your neck, tattoos, tight pants, earrings and matching shoes that look like carpet! I took this photo of Bon Jovi's Jon Bon Jovi and Ritchie Sambora at a press conference to promote their 1993 Keep The Faith Australian tour.

Bon Jovi have a huge fan base and every time they tour Australia they have an enormous amount of mainly female fans waiting for them everywhere they go. If you can get to them they are usually pretty fan-friendly—all I can say is, good luck getting to them. A lot of security plus a lot of fans equals a major problem. It's not impossible though—try the hotel's bar after one of their shows.

Madonna 1993

In 1993, Madonna toured Australia for the first and only time. When she arrived in Sydney there was about 40 fans, 30 press, ten policemen and ten security guards all trying either to meet her, photograph her or protect her. At one stage the police put up barricades outside the hotel that she was staying in to keep fans and media at a distance.

The day she arrived in Sydney I went down to the hotel with two friends. We realised that she wouldn't come out of the front of the hotel so we went around the back. As we got to the back of the hotel we noticed two security guards waiting at a staff door looking very anxious and nervous. A minute later the staff door swung open and out came Madonna. Her security team pushed all three of us out of the way and started to jog up the street. We were the only three who knew that she had left the hotel.

My friend was a huge Madonna fan and desperately wanted her autograph, so we got in the car and drove down the road and watched as they ran down to Bondi Beach. We waited for her to jog past us on her return to the hotel, basically just out of curiosity. As she was about to pass my car, my friend said to me, 'Rich, I'm going to run up to her and ask her to sign my programme.' She got out of the car and ran across the road to Madonna, programme and pen in hand. The security freaked out and started yelling and waving their hands at this single fan. I snapped this photo at the precise moment it was all happening. Madonna didn't sign the programme but she did have a smile on her face at my friend's enthusiasm.

Nick Cave 1993

Singer/songwriter Nick Cave is dark, mysterious and really cool; so cool that my idol Michael Hutchence wanted to be just like him. Hutchence liked the idea of being an underground musician and that's exactly what Nick Cave is. I took this photo at a hotel just down the road from Sydney's red light district in January 1993 when Nick was back in his home country to perform some shows. Maybe Bono got the idea to wear dark sunglasses once he saw Nick Cave looking so cool in a pair?

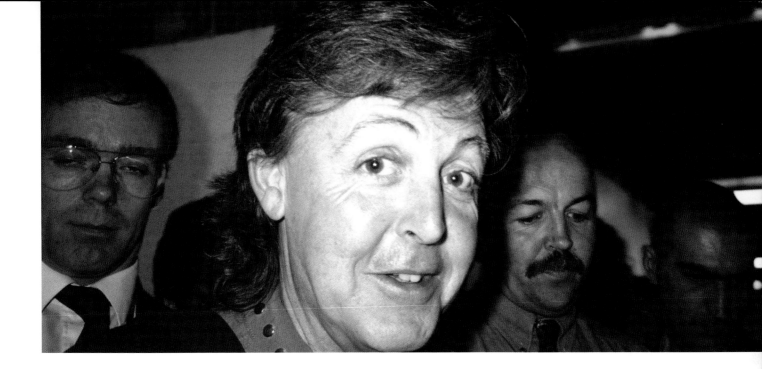

Paul McCartney 1993

You know when people ask you if there is one thing in your life you would change? Well, mine is that I would have had a photo taken with Paul McCartney when I met him in 1993. Paul was in Sydney to do some concerts for his world tour. The first day he was in town he went to do a radio interview. When the interview was over he went out the back of the station surrounded by about six hefty security guards. My friend and I and another fan were waiting at the back for his autograph. When he came out of the radio station he noticed three of us waiting for him and walked over to us, he signed our items but was told by the security team that he had to go. I asked him if I could take his photo and he said, 'Yeah sure' but his security didn't want me to take it.

I put the camera up to my face and snapped it just as he was getting shoved past by six hot-headed security guards. The expression on his face sums up the moment perfectly. He looks like a school kid being told by his parents that he has to go, but being a bit cheeky snuck in a pose without his parents knowing. The next few nights after his concerts, Paul and Linda would come back to their hotel and sign autographs and pose for photos for all of the fans. I never asked for a photo with him. In 2001 while living in London I tried to meet him again, this time there were about 200 fans waiting for him to arrive at a stage door. He had no choice but to quickly rush in to the venue. Paul, if you're reading this—I would love another opportunity for that photo with you.

Carl Lewis 1994

I took this photo of athlete Carl Lewis in 1994 when he was in Sydney to attend a charity dinner. When I arrived at the dinner I noticed that most of the photographers were all waiting inside for Carl to arrive. I also noticed that the sun had just set and the sky on that particular night looked very beautiful. As I was admiring the sky a stretch limousine pulled up out the front of the function and out got Carl Lewis. Armed only with my $90 camera I snapped this photo of him—he hadn't even finished doing up his suit jacket. I not only captured one of the greatest athletes of all time but I captured a small slice of Sydney's beautiful sky. It just goes to show that you don't need a fancy camera to take a nice shot.

George Bush and John Newcombe 1994

In 1994 my girlfriend and I were at a charity tennis match in Sydney to watch some celebrities and former tennis greats play a fun day of tennis to raise money for sick kids.

My girlfriend walked passed former world tennis champion John Newcombe and heard (very cleverly) that the next day he was going to be playing a game of tennis with the former President of the United States at that particular tennis venue. I walked over to Newcombe and asked him if the story was true and he told me that it was. I hadn't even heard that former US president George Bush was in the country. So the next day I went down to the tennis courts and hung around for an hour or so.

I noticed that the staff had closed the main gates to the venue and a short time later a motor parade with police escort arrived at the tennis court. Bush got out of the car with Newcombe. I was the only one in the stadium. His security/secret service came straight over to me and asked what I was doing. I told them that John Newcombe had told me that he was going to be playing tennis here and I was told to come down here to take some photos. Now I didn't tell them who told me to come down to take the photos—that was actually my girlfriend. But they didn't know that and I wasn't going to tell them.

The US secret service guys asked me to take everything out of my pockets and show them some identification. I quickly did both, they checked me out and gave me the all-clear to take a few photos. After a nervous few minutes I took a few photos of both men just having a talk and one photo of George hitting the ball. In fact a ball came straight over to where I was sitting and George walked over to me and politely asked for the ball back. Never in my wildest dreams did I think that I would be throwing a tennis ball at the former president, but I did. He thanked me for the ball and a moment later his security told me to leave. I certainly wasn't going to argue against that request as I was outnumbered twenty to one. How many people can say they have thrown a tennis ball at the former president of the United States and live to tell the tale?

Kylie Minogue 1994

This photo of Kylie is one of my favourite photos of her since first meeting her in 1989. Kylie was at St Vincent's Hospital in Sydney in 1994 to meet with AIDS patients. The day was rainy and cold so the hospital staff gave Kylie an umbrella while she went outside to pose for photos near a tree that had ribbons on it to represent World AIDS Day. After posing for the media, Kylie then went into the hospital where she spent a few hours with her very sick but adoring fans.

Prince Charles 1994

In 1994 Prince Charles visited Sydney as one of his official royal duties. Everywhere he went hundreds of well-wishers warmly greeted the Prince. My friend and I were trying to get a few decent photos of Charles while he was in town. On one of the days he was in Sydney he left a Naval base and cruised across Sydney Harbour.

My friend and I stood on some rocks with a bunch of other royal watchers and yelled out to Charles as he went passed us. I snapped a few photos and hoped for the best. When I got the film developed I was surprised that I got this photo of him looking directly down my lens. And for those of you playing 'Royal Trivia' at home, the boat that Charles crossed the harbour in was the *Girralong*.

Tony Curtis 1994

Actor Tony Curtis is definitely one of the nicest people in showbiz that I have ever met. I know this because I have been lucky to meet him on a number of occasions in Sydney and in LA and he is always great to the fans. This photo of Tony and me was taken in 1994 when he was in Sydney to promote his autobiography. When a visiting celebrity is in town to promote a book they usually only sign the book that they have come out to promote; Tony not only signed books but anything else that was put in front of him. In fact he spent so long signing autographs and speaking to fans that the staff at the hotel where he was doing his speech about his book actually had to ask him to leave the area because they had another function that day. Tony left the function room and continued to spend time with his adoring fans in the lobby of the hotel. I wish they were all like Tony Curtis!

Bryan Ferry 1995

These two photos of musician Bryan Ferry show you exactly why I would rather meet a celebrity at their hotel than after a show with a bunch of other fans. Usually after a show or concert at a theatre a number of fans wait at the stage door for the performer to leave. The fans usually wait for an autograph or a photo or even just to see their idol up close.

In the first of these two photos, Ferry is exiting the stage door and being mobbed by dozens of well-wishers. The other photo I took at his hotel only moments after. As you can see Ferry is much more relaxed, which enabled me to get a better photo of him.

Courtney Love 1995

Courtney came out to Australia in 1995 for a music festival called the Big Day Out with her band Hole. When she arrived at Sydney Airport I was there with about five other fans. Courtney signed my T-shirt without me asking her to. I asked her to stop as it was an INXS T-shirt and I didn't want her name on it. Courtney told me that she didn't give a fu*k if it was an INXS T-shirt.

After the autograph signing inside the airport Courtney and fellow musician Evan Dando went outside for a smoke and to chill out. While they were relaxing a fan gave Courtney a scrap folder with newspaper clippings of her late husband's (Kurt Cobain) suicide. Courtney sat on the ground for about ten minutes and looked through the newspaper clippings. In this photo you can see that Courtney is looking at one of these articles.

Sir Donald Bradman 1995

This photo of Sir Donald Bradman and me is my favourite photo of all those taken with celebrities. Sir Donald is the greatest cricketing batsman the world has ever seen. It has been statistically proven by university scholars that Sir Donald was the greatest athlete the world has ever seen. Better than Babe Ruth, Joe DiMaggio, Michael Jordan and Tiger Woods. To many of us Sir Donald Bradman was almost like a myth. We had all heard of him but only a few ever met him.

In 1995 while at the Grand Prix in Adelaide I went to Sir Donald's house and simply knocked on his door. A lady answered the door and I asked if I could meet Sir Donald. She told me that just before I came to the house a group of school children visited the house because they were doing a school project on Sir Donald and they asked him if he could give them a hand. Sir Donald spent over 30 minutes with the children helping them with their project.

This is the only photo in my entire collection that I have had enlarged and it proudly hangs in my office. When I told people in 1995 that I was going to meet 'the Don' they laughed at me. This photo proved to me that even the impossible is sometimes possible.

Sir Donald Bradman 1995

Sometimes I question why I go out and try to have my photo taken with celebrities and then I look at my photos of Sir Donald Bradman and it all makes sense. In 1995 after I had simply knocked on his door, Sir Donald greeted me at the door and I asked him if he could sign some items for me. He took the items from me and sat on the front steps of his house. Afterwards I asked him for directions to a part of Adelaide that I didn't know. He told me that he was heading out in the same direction and suggested that I follow him. While I was behind him in my car, we drove through a school where there was a group of school children practising cricket in the nets. Sir Donald stopped his car and watched the children as they practised. If only they'd known that Sir Donald Bradman was watching them play cricket!

Elle Macpherson 1995

I used to see Elle all the time in the early 1990s at a Sydney hotel but never bothered to get a photo with her. I had met her in 1992 but only took a photo of her. On this particular day in 1995, Elle and her then partner Tim Jeffreys were having a leisurely day off in Elle's home town of Sydney. A friend of mine called me and told me that he just saw Elle going into a restaurant for lunch. I remembered that I needed a photo with her so I went down to the restaurant. When Elle came out of the restaurant I asked her for a photo and she happily obliged. As I was having my photo taken with her a guy drove past and noticed Elle. He slammed on his brakes and jumped out of his car—he couldn't believe his luck. He was so star struck that he asked her if she would sign the front of his car. Elle gave him a smile and signed his car with a thick black pen. I wonder if the guy ever got his car washed.

Esther Williams 1995

Hollywood legend Esther Williams came to Sydney in 1995 to attend a benefit lunch for
Australia's very own Olympic swimming legend, Dawn Fraser. When she arrived in Sydney Esther did a press
conference to promote the lunch to honour Dawn. These were still the good old days for me when the airline that the star flew
and the hotel where the star was staying at used to be promoted; now these details are secret. In the early to mid 1990s the hotel
where the star stayed at used to put up their name at the press conference behind the star so it would get published in the paper.
If I didn't know where the star was staying and I missed the press conference I would simply check out the paper the following
day and I would instantly know where to wait.

   After the press conference I had this photo taken with the Hollywood legend and asked her to sign an original movie poster
that showed her alongside another Hollywood legend, Cyd Charisse. Esther was admiring the original poster and pointed out to
me that Cyd Charisse had one of the best pair of legs in Hollywood.

George Harrison 1995

In 1995 I was working as a photographer at the last Grand Prix that was held in Adelaide. I was informed by a friend that George Harrison was staying at the Hilton Hotel. The hotel lobby was full of Beatles fans, all waiting for George to arrive. I took this photo as he was getting into the lift. George had an amazing memory for people he had met in the past. If George met you the previous year and signed an autograph for you he would remember you the following year. George was very good to his fans.

One particular year at the Adelaide Grand Prix my friend had a VW van waiting outside George's hotel that had the Beatles' faces painted on it. George came out of the hotel, posed for a photo in front of the van and then accepted a lift to the Grand Prix in the van. When my friend arrived at the security check point at the Grand Prix the security guard wouldn't let him in. My friend told the guy that he had George Harrison in the van sitting next to him. The security guard told him to leave, then George leaned across the front of the driver's seat and said, 'I'm George Harrison'. The guard instantly let the former Beatle drive straight on through. I would have loved to have seen that guard's face when he saw George Harrison sitting in the painted van. Can you imagine?

Halle Berry 1995

I took this photo of actor Halle while she was at Maroubra Beach in Sydney. She was in Sydney with fellow actor Jim Belushi to film the movie *Race to the Sun*. Halle was almost unknown then so when I was going through my negatives for this book I was surprised that I had even taken any photos of her. I wish I had asked for her autograph as last year in 2006 she was in the top ten worst celebrity autograph signers. It would have been interesting to see if she would have signed back in 1995.

Harold Larwood 1995

Bodyline cricketer Harold Larwood became the most hated person in Australia in 1932–33 due to his bowling style known as Bodyline. Strangely enough he ended up moving to Australia in the 1950s and spent the rest of his life happily living in Sydney. I first met Harold in 1994 after I came across his name in the telephone book. I rang him up and he invited me over to his house. Harold was a very kind person with a cheeky personality. I was very fortunate to get to know him and I spent many hours with him in his Kensington home where he told me numerous stories about his playing days.

The last conversation I had with him, he told me that he still received fan mail from around the world. He considered himself to be 50 per cent English and 50 per cent Australian. The ball that Harold is holding in this photo is one of the balls that he used in the infamous Bodyline series.

Jerry Hall 1995

In 1995 the Rolling Stones toured Australia. They had not been to Australia for a number of years so when they came to Sydney there were a number of fans and media waiting for them at their hotel. Model Jerry Hall, who was Mick Jagger's wife at the time, used to leave the hotel every day with their children and take in the sights of Sydney. This photo is of Jerry Hall and then teenager Elisabeth Jagger. Elisabeth is now all grown up and has become a successful model herself.

I have got a friend who not only has his photo taken with celebrities but also their children. He tells me he gets the kids' photos just in case they become famous—maybe he's onto something.

Keanu Reeves 1995

Actor Keanu Reeves came out to Australia in 1995 with his band Dogstar. Keanu, who is the bassist in the band, attracted a lot of female fans at his Sydney hotel. One night after one of their gigs Keanu came back to his hotel just as a bride and groom arrived. Keanu kindly posed with the couple before getting mobbed by a number of screaming girls.

He was so hard to get a photo with at the hotel that I went to the airport and met him by myself away from the screaming girls. The only problem was I had no-one to take the photo of the two of us, so I asked a passer-by to take the photo. This elderly gentleman said to Keanu and me, 'Okay ready 1, 2, 3'. He took the photo and told Keanu that he wasn't smiling. It was a funny moment.

Kevin Costner 1995

Kevin came to Sydney in 1995 to promote his epic flop *Waterworld*. In 1995 Kevin Costner was still a huge movie star so any photos of him were in demand.

During a press conference to promote his movie he said that after the press conference he was going to play a game of golf. In Sydney there are only a handful of golf courses that the rich and famous play at. My friend and I took a guess and found Kevin at a particular course. We asked him if we could get our photo taken with him as we couldn't get one at the press conference. He turned down our request but said that we could take a few photos of him on the first hole. I took this photo of him just before he teed off. He had left his phone on and was having a humorous conversation on the course. I took a few shots and then we were asked to leave him alone.

My friend was a big fan of Costner's and really wanted the photo with him so he followed Costner to the next hole. Costner asked my friend to come over to him, gave him the photo and then asked him to leave. I couldn't believe my friend had the nerves to follow him to the next hole. In 1995 this was a prized photo to have. In 2007 …

Michael Schumacher 1995

In 1995 I went and photographed the last Grand Prix that was to be held in Adelaide. The winner of that year's race was British driver Damon Hill. The morning after the race the media and fans all waited outside the drivers' hotel to see them leaving. Damon Hill wasn't the friendliest person in the world; he only stopped for the media briefly and would only sign a few autographs for waiting fans.

In contrast Michael Schumacher was fantastic. There were before his Ferrari days and his profile was not as it is today. He spoke to the media for over twenty minutes and after interviews he signed autographs for all of the waiting fans. There was such a buzz back in 1995 about Schumacher, even though Hill won the race.

Morgan Freeman 1995

I had heard that actor Morgan was in Sydney to promote a movie so my friend and I went down to the hotel where he was staying and noticed that he was in between interviews. I walked up to him and asked if I could take a photo of him while he was just relaxing. 'Sure you can,' replied a calm Freeman. Just as I was about to take his photo his PR ran over to me and told me I wasn't allowed to take it. She demanded that I tell her who I worked for and how I got into the hotel. I calmly informed the girl that the hotel had doors and that was my way in and that I worked for a photo agency. The girl was making a real fuss.

Freeman told her that it was fine with him. The photo took all of about two seconds and I thanked Freeman for his time and patience and wished him good luck. He looked up at me and then looked at the PR girl and then back at me and gave me a wink. It's an interesting photo of Morgan—I wasn't aware that he had a brace on his right leg.

Phil Collins 1995

Musician Phil Collins toured Australia in 1995 for his *But Seriously* world tour. I took this photo of Phil during a press conference to promote the tour. Up until the late 1990s press conferences were usually very relaxed and sometimes even fun. In 2000 the celebrity phenomenon went to another level and photographing and meeting celebrities became more of a chore. This, however, was a fun press conference. The promoter was clever enough to give Phil a didgeridoo to play and the media captured the moment—a perfectly set-up photo opportunity.

Pierce Brosnan 1995

Pierce came out to Australia to promote his first James Bond movie *Golden Eye*. When I went to his hotel to meet him he was just coming back from a day out on Sydney Harbour. I asked him to sign an autograph for me, and he kindly did.

   After he signed his name on my poster he asked me how much I was going to sell his autograph for. I told him that I didn't sell autographs and no-one else in Australia did either—this was before eBay. Pierce told me that he was recently in an autograph store in New York and his autograph was selling for only $70 while Barbara Streisand's autograph was selling for $250. Pierce told me that he better start making some more movies so his autograph would be worth more. The photo that I got with him was amusing as he made a gun shape figure out of his hand and pretended to shoot me like he was James Bond.

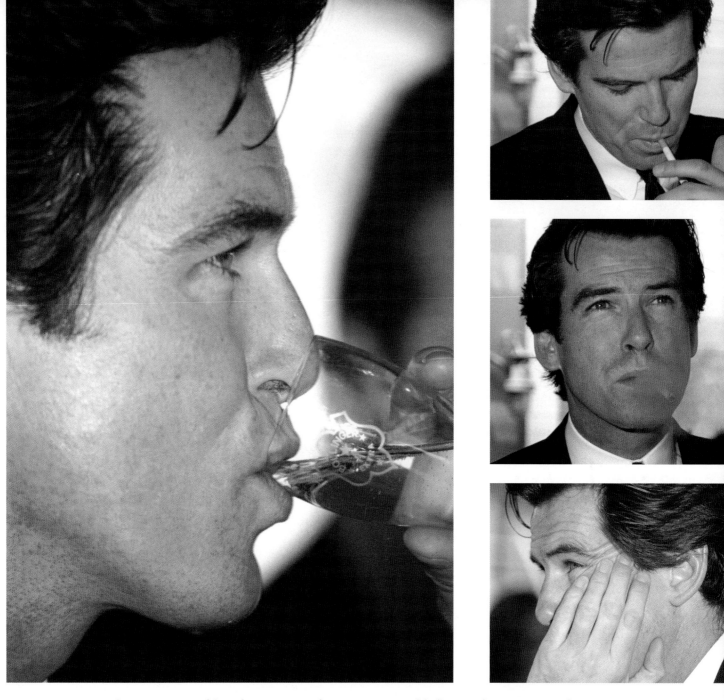

Pierce Brosnan at his Sydney press conference to promot his first movie as James Bond.

Prince Edward 1995

Prince Edward was in Adelaide in 1995 for the city's very last Grand Prix. This photo proves that royals do not discriminate when it comes to signing autographs for their loyal servants. I took this photo of Edward when he was leaving his hotel to go and attend a day at the Grand Prix.

A young girl was waiting for the drivers to leave the hotel so she could get her programme signed. When Edward left the hotel the girl asked him to sign her programme; he gave her a forced smile and walked straight passed her. British royals are not allowed to sign autographs, only official papers, birthday cards, Christmas cards, guest books and the like. Would signing this girl's programme really have ruined his day? He could have at least shaken her hand—isn't that what royals do?

Angus Young 1996

I took this photo of band member Angus when
AC/DC came home to Australia to play some gigs as
part of their world tour. Because Angus has a house
in Sydney he doesn't stay at a hotel when he is in
town, so I took this photo of him at the back of the
Sydney Entertainment Centre when he arrived for a
sound check. Angus is always very good to the fans
and always has time for an autograph a photo and a
chat. This photo reminds me of their song 'Jail Break'
because of the bars.

Charlie Sheen 1996

Charlie came to Sydney in 1996 as one of the guests that came to town to open the movie themed restaurant Planet Hollywood. Charlie wasn't the only Hollywood celebrity that was in town to open the restaurant, there was also Bruce Willis, Jean-Claude Van Dame, Sylvester Stallone, Danny Glover, Jackie Chan and supermodel Cindy Crawford.

With a guest list like this you can only imagine the amount of media and fans that were waiting for a glimpse of these stars. The first few days that they were all in town I had exams for a photographic course that I was doing, so my time spent at the hotel was minimal. I got a tip-off that Charlie was going to Planet Hollywood for some lunch, and I waited out the front of the restaurant for him to arrive. When he did the security tried to rush him in but I was lucky to get this quick photo before they did.

Charlie ended up being really cool. On the day that he checked out of his hotel he spent over 15 minutes signing autographs for all of the fans waiting for him.

Charlton Heston 1996

I get asked all the time which celebs are the nastiest/rudest to deal with. Actor Charlton Heston falls into the not-very-nice category. I was in Melbourne on a holiday when I got a tip-off that Charlton was flying in on a particular day to promote his autobiography. I went to the airport but when he got off the flight he was in a terrible mood. I asked him if he would sign an original *Ben Hur* movie programme and he simply ignored me. I then asked him if I could have my photo taken with him. He told me that he doesn't do photos. I then asked him again if he would please sign my programme. Charlton then turned around and said, 'Listen, son, I'm here to sign my book and nothing else.'

I then said to him, 'If I can't have an autograph then can I have a photo walking next to you?' He didn't say yes or no so I walked next to him and my girlfriend snapped a photo. When I had the film processed I was very disappointed to see that he had turned his face away on purpose.

Chris Isaak 1996

I've only ever met musician Chris Isaak once and I don't have anything bad to say about him, unlike a few of my friends who have tried to meet him over the years and have got nothing. In 1996 Chris was in town to attend the Australian Record Industry Awards, the ARIAs. When he arrived in Sydney he had a twisted ankle so it was strapped up, which limited his ability to walk.

On the night of the ARIAs Chris had to walk from one hall to another. I noticed him hobbling along and asked him if he needed a hand. He happily took up my offer and allowed my girlfriend to take this photo of us walking to the awards.

Cindy Crawford 1996

Supermodel Cindy Crawford was in town to attend the opening of a Planet Hollywood restaurant with a few other international celebrities. On one of the days that she was in town Cindy was shopping at Sydney's famous Bondi Beach. I got a phone call from a friend of mine letting me know that she was down there. I went to Bondi with a few of my mates and we saw Cindy straightaway. None of us wanted to bother her so we just drove past her in the street. As we were driving past we saw that a guy with a guitar had also noticed the supermodel and he walked up to her and started to serenade her. I'll give Cindy credit; she saw the funny side of it and just went on shopping. I went back to the hotel with my friends to see if we could get a photo with her when she arrived but she was rushed into the hotel by security.

However, my luck changed on the night after the restaurant opening when Cindy arrived back at her hotel and allowed me and a few other waiting fans one photo each with her. The following day I was back at the hotel waiting for the other celebrities to check out. A few fans were waiting for Cindy to leave—when she did she wouldn't give anyone a photo saying that if she gives a photo to one person she would have to give one to everyone else. It was a valid excuse, but there were only two people waiting for her that morning, the rest of us had got her the night before and didn't need her again.

As they say, you've got to be in the right place at the right time.

Crowded House 1996

In 1996 one of Australia's favourite bands, Crowded House, played their very last gig on the steps of the Sydney Opera House. The day before the gig they did a sound check and some media interviews to thank their fans for all of their love and support. I took this photo as they were doing one of these interviews. Sadly drummer Paul Hester committed suicide in 2005, which was a huge blow to the music world and all of Paul's fans both in Australia and around the world.

Neil Finn, Nick Seymour and Paul Hester were just the nicest bunch of guys that you could ever meet—famous or not. Although I never got a group photo with them I did get individual photos and I have some great memories of spending a few days with these guys.

Danny DeVito 1996

Pint-sized actor Danny came out to Australia in 1996 to promote his movie *Matilda*. My friend and I were waiting for him to leave the hotel one day when out came the hotel's security. He informed us that we were not allowed to ask DeVito for an autograph or a photo and that he would call the police if we didn't leave. Now, because I have been doing this for a number of years I know that the police can't do anything to you if you are standing on a public footpath waiting for an autograph.

I asked the security guy if he could please call the police because I wanted to see his face when they turned up. He started to almost panic as he knew that the visiting Hollywood star was about to come out. I had to tell him to calm down—all we were going to do was politely ask DeVito for an autograph and a photo. If he said yes then great, if he doesn't want to do it, then no problem we would simply leave.

About ten minutes or so later DeVito came out of the hotel and the security guy tried his very hardest to block us from asking him for a photo or autograph. His attempt to stop us backfired as DeVito walked over to us and shook our hand, then signed our autographs and posed for this photo.

After DeVito left my friend and I started to walk back to our car, but the security guy followed us and tried to stop us leaving by standing in front of the car, telling us that we were going to follow DeVito and he had to protect the star. This was so ridiculous that all we could do was laugh. We informed the security guard that DeVito had long gone and we just wanted to go home. This guy really just had to let it go. Not surprisingly he appeared in the background of our photo. Let's hope he's gotten over it by now.

Denzel Washington 1996

I met actor Denzel Washington at a press conference while he was in Sydney to promote the
movie *Courage Under Fire*. After the press conference my friend Miles and I had a photo taken with him.
He seemed very friendly and easygoing and was in a very good mood at the press conference. That night another friend
waited for him to leave a restaurant, but Denzel told him that he doesn't do autographs or photos when he's not working.

   This is why I used to go to a lot of press conferences—celebrities think of a press conference as working and while you are
working you are obligated to the media and sometimes the fans. It's all about timing and a bit of luck.

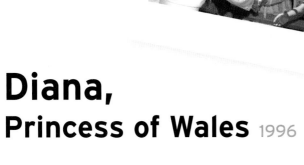

Diana,
Princess of Wales 1996

I took this photo of Diana when she was visiting
Sydney for a charity event. On this particular day,
Diana was visiting patients at St Vincent's Hospital.
A large crowd of admirers and just as many media
were waiting for a glimpse of her.

When Diana left the hospital she walked around and
met the crowd, which included a few of Sydney's drag
queens. Like everyone else I was trying to get a great
photo of Diana. As she came closer to me I went under
the barricades and walked with Diana for 30 seconds
or so. Let's just say I wasn't in the police department's
good books, but I did get some great photos.

Dimebag Darrell 1996

In the early to mid 1990s I really got into heavy metal music. In 1996 Pantera toured Australia and my friends and I went down to the hotel they were staying at to meet them. All four members were really cool about signing autographs for us. One night in between concerts, band member Dimebag and a few of the band's crew spent a night boozing up at Kings Cross. Their hotel was just down the road so we waited for Dimebag to come back. About 1am a stumbling but happy Dimebag walked down the road towards the hotel. My friends and I went up to him and he signed our items and posed for this photo.

Sadly in December 2004 while Dimebag was playing on stage with his new band Damageplan, a crazed Pantera fan got up on stage and shot him dead. When I heard this news I looked through my photo albums and realised that I didn't have a photo of with him so I went through my Pantera negatives and found this one. Ironically Dimebag was the only member from Pantera who I got a photo with.

Jackie Chan 1996

Jackie was filming a movie about four hours north of Sydney. I went up to the film set and watched the day's filming, which included blowing up a large farmhouse. After the day of filming I left the set just before Jackie did and drove into the small town where they were staying. Lucky for me there was only one hotel in the town so it wasn't too hard to work out where he was staying.

   He arrived shortly after I did and walked over to me. I asked him if I could have my photo taken with him, and he agreed to. But he wouldn't let my friend take the photo; he insisted that his female assistant take the photo. Who was I to argue with this martial arts expert? After the photo he took my items inside his hotel room and signed them with his pen. He signs his autograph in English and Chinese. It's actually a very elegant signature.

James Brown 1996

'I feel good!' That's what musician James Brown kept yelling out at Sydney Airport after he finished his press conference to promote his concert tour of Australia in 1996. As he was walking and singing in the airport I asked him for a photo; he turned around and yelled out, 'I feel good and so does he.' And I did.

After the photo James signed a photo for me with a huge smile on his face and also wrote: 'I feel good. James Brown'. He then walked over to his waiting limousine and screamed out, yep you guessed it, 'I feel good!'

Jason and Jaymz 1996
Metallica

Like millions of people around the world in the 1990s I was a huge fan of Metallica. I have met them a few times over the years when they have come to Sydney and they are always really cool with the fans. When a band comes to town I always try to get a group photo with them. This is nearly almost impossible, so when I got my photo with two of four members from Metallica I was extremely happy. It's a good photo to have because Jason, who used to play bass in the band, has now left Metallica.

Jimmy Page 1996

I wasn't too sure how Led Zeppelin band member Jimmy Page would be when I met him as so many people consider him to be a rock god, and some rock gods aren't the nicest people to meet. But I had no such problem with Jimmy.

Robert Plant and Jimmy Page toured Australia in 1996. They had not toured Australia since the 1970s, so their Australian tour was a huge event for all Zeppelin fans. Strangely enough there were only a few fans waiting at the hotel for them and they were German fans who were following their heroes around the globe.

I got this photo with Jimmy after he came back from one of their sold-out gigs. A rock god and a very cool guy; what more could you ask for.

Johnny Rotten 1996

Though I wasn't a huge fan of the Sex Pistols I really wanted to meet them when they toured Australia in 1996. I spent about two days at their hotel and had met three out of the four members. The only one I didn't see was front man Johnny Rotten. I found out on the last day that he wasn't staying with the other three members of the band. He was in a different hotel all together.

I went to the airport the day that they were leaving and saw this guy walking around the airport with his hair spiked up, coloured green and gold (the sporting colours of Australia). I knew this guy wasn't an Australian sporting fan so it must have been Johnny. I was a little nervous walking up to him but I had nothing to worry about. He was fantastic and gave me this photo and signed a few autographs for me and my friend. He did catch the same flight as the other members of the Pistols.

Kiefer Sutherland 1996

Actor Kiefer Sutherland came out to Australia in 1996 to film the movie *Dark City*. He stayed in a rented house and it proved impossible to meet him. A few months after the movie had finished filming Kiefer was needed back in Sydney for a few more days work. This time he was staying in a hotel and I found out which one it was. After two days of waiting for him and not seeing anything I decided to call him at the hotel just to see if he was still there. I rang the hotel and he was not only staying there but he was checked in under his own name. He answered the phone and I firstly apologised for calling him but added that I had been outside his hotel for two days and I just wanted to know if it was at all possible to meet him.

To my utter surprise Kiefer apologised for not coming out, telling me that he had been sick for the last couple of days and that he wasn't leaving his room on this particular day as well. He did say that he was going to go for a walk tomorrow at 10am and if that was all right with me he would meet me then. The following day I went down to the hotel and Kiefer came out at 10am. He apologised again for keeping me waiting for a few days and then gave me a photo with him. He's certainly one of my favourites and one of the nicest celebrities I have ever met.

Kylie Minogue 1996

During the mid 1990s Kylie's career hit a bit of a brick wall. She had just released an album called *Impossible Princess,* which was a critical success but not a commercial success. Her fans, though extremely loyal, were not supporting the 'pop princess' as much as they had in previous years. So this was the best time for me to meet her.

In 1995 Kylie did a duet with fellow Aussie Nick Cave. Nick was touring with the Big Day Out and Kylie was joining him on stage just for this song. Her profile had dropped somewhat and there were no fans or media following her around. The night after she performed her song with Nick, she and her boyfriend were chasing each other outside their hotel. I was in shock as I had never seen Kylie so relaxed. I went into the hotel to wait for her and a moment later she came running into the hotel's lobby.

She noticed me sitting on a lounge and came over with a huge smile and a hug. She was still laughing and playing around with her boyfriend. We got a few photos sitting on the couch together and then I took this one of her sitting on the couch. This is my favourite photo ever taken of Kylie. And it's one of Kylie's favourites as well—every time I show her the photo she asks me for a copy of it. I have shown it to her about five times and yep she's now got five copies of it. She looks so innocent in the photo—there's no make-up, no stylist, it's just Kylie. I doubt I'll have the chance to take a photo like this again.

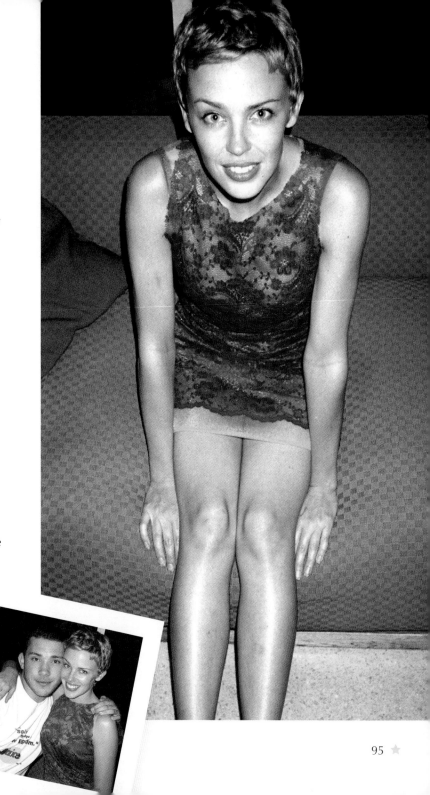

Linda Evangelista 1996

When Linda came out to Sydney in 1996 it was right in the middle of the 'supermodel frenzy'. She attended a function at the Hilton Hotel and arrived surrounded by five security guards. On her way into the function I couldn't get anywhere near her because of her security team. I stuck around until the function had finished and tried to ask her for a photo but I was pushed back by her overprotective security. As I was trying to explain to one of her beefed-up security guards that I just wanted a photo with her, Linda, who was just about to get on the escalator and leave, turned around and said, 'Hang on a moment. This guy wants his photo with me.' She turned around and posed for this photo. Not a lot of celebrities go against their security, as they are usually outnumbered and sometimes intimidated by these oversized goons. Thank God Linda had the guts to defy them.

Michael Jackson 1996

Michael was in Sydney in 1996 to do some concerts. The hotel was full of Jackson fans 24 hours a day. On the final day he was in Sydney I went down to his hotel wearing a casual suit and holding a laptop computer. I walked into the hotel and up to the first floor. Once there I sat down and worked on the computer. After 30 minutes or so one of Michael's security guards cleared the entire floor. He noticed that I was working on the computer and did not bother me. A few minutes later Jackson walked out of the lifts and headed in my direction, where there were a few children waiting with their parents to meet him. Michael happily signed autographs for the children and posed for photos. After he had spent time with the children I casually walked up to him and asked for a photo. Michael simply nodded his head and put out his arm so I could stand next to him.

He walked down the stairs and signed as many autographs as he could for his devoted fans. I remember when I got the film developed I couldn't stop looking at the photo of Michael and me. I mean, Michael Jackson! And me!

Neil Diamond 1996

Singer/songwriter Neil Diamond toured Australia in 1996 and did a press conference to promote the tour in front of the Sydney Opera House. The media were all waiting for Neil to arrive when all of a sudden we all heard the roar of about ten Harley Davidson's driving into the front area of the Opera House. Neil who is an avid Harley Davidson enthusiast had spent the day roaring around Sydney on a Harley with a few mates. Neil posed for some photos for the media with his Harley and was soaking up the beautiful day out the front of the Opera House.

I took a few shots for my agency and then I thought that I needed something different. I stood behind Neil and yelled out to him. The plan worked. Neil looked back in my direction and I got this photo of him that was completely different from the other photographers' photos. I wasn't too popular with the other photographers, however, as I ended up in everyone else's photo—just look at their faces. What's the point of all standing around a celebrity and all getting the same photo?

Olivia Newton-John 1996

Call me precious but I don't like taking the same photo as the rest of the photographers, so most of the time, the only reason I attend a media photo call is to have my photo taken with a celebrity. On this occasion Olivia was at the opening of the IMAX cinema in Sydney. When she arrived the media all gathered in front of her while she happily posed for photos. I quickly left the area where the photographers were taking their photos and walked behind Olivia to try to get a different photo from the rest of the photographers. I yelled out to her and got this photo with the rest of the photographers as my backdrop.

Today in 2007 there would be double the photographers that you can see in this photograph.

Paul Hogan 1996

Now you would think that getting a photo with Australia's very own Paul Hogan would be easy, but Paul doesn't live in Australia, he lives in LA, and very rarely makes public appearances in Australia. So when 'Hoges' came out to Sydney in 1996 to promote the movie *Flipper* I jumped at the opportunity to try to meet him.

I waited with a friend of mine at his hotel for him to come back from the movie premiere. When he did I walked up to him and asked him for a photo. The doorman of the hotel didn't like that I was meeting his hotel's VIP guest so he ran over to Hoges and told him that I was a professional. I told Hoges that all I wanted was a photo with him; what could I be a professional at? Hogan looked at the doorman like he was an idiot and gave me a few friendly photos with him.

After the photos Hoges patted me on the back and said, 'Don't worry, mate. That guy's a professional door opener.' Hoges gave me a cheeky grin and walked back into the hotel. The 'professional door opener' ordered me off the hotel's property, which didn't bother me a single bit; Hoges' joke made the doorman look like a professional idiot.

Perry Farrell 1996

I first met Perry in the early 1990s when he was in Sydney to perform some shows with his band Jane's Addiction. When I met him in the early 1990s Perry wouldn't let me take any photos of him. He would only sign one autograph for each fan waiting for him at his hotel. To say the least he was very, very strange.

Then I met him again in 1996 when he was fronting a band called Porno For Pyros. On this occasion Perry could not have been any nicer or relaxed. He posed for photos, signed autographs and even spent time talking with the fans. I think it must have taken him a few years to get used to being famous. Thank God he did. He's even smiling in this photo.

Priscilla Presley 1996

The ex-wife of Elvis Presley came out to Sydney to promote a perfume range that she created in 1996. The day that actress/entrepreneur Priscilla arrived she had a full day of media obligations. One of these media obligations was appearing on a top rating radio show. My friend and I waited for her to leave the station, but there was one problem. Priscilla had a team of six security guards looking after her—guys in dark suits with walkie talkies. When she left the studios she noticed that we were waiting for her, so she kindly walked straight over to us and asked if we wanted her to sign anything for us. She signed her autographs and we each had a a photo with her.

The next day I was at her press conference to photograph her for my photo agency. After the conference I asked Priscilla if she could sign a piece of cardboard that had her name printed on it. As she was signing it the PR girl came running over and said to her that it was the only thing that they had printed up with her name on it and she couldn't sign it for me. Priscilla said to the girl: 'I'm sure you guys can print another one of these for me,' and continued to sign the item for me.

After she left the PR demanded the autograph back. I showed the girl that Priscilla had signed it 'To Richard Love Priscilla Presley'. She realised that it was no longer any use to her and stormed off.

Robert Plant 1996

Led Zeppelin musician Robert Plant was having breakfast with Jimmy Page in Sydney's prestigious suburb of Double Bay. Both of these music legends were in town to do some gigs. I went down to the hotel one morning and noticed that they were having breakfast across the road. As Robert was walking back to his hotel I asked if I could take a photo of him.

He asked me why I wanted to take a photo of him for. I told him that he was a legend of the 1970s and that I enjoyed his music. He then said to me that he can't understand why after all these years people were still interested in him. As he was about to walk across the street he opened his arms and told me to take the photo.

Robert Wagner 1996

When I was a kid the television show *Hart to Hart* was my favourite show. So in 1996 when Robert Wagner and Stephanie Powers came out to Sydney to film a television movie of *Hart to Hart*, I was very excited .The only problem was how to meet them. I had read in the paper that they were filming the show in and around the city of Sydney. So I thought with a bit of luck or a tip-off I would bump into them, and that's exactly what happened.

I was at a hotel in the city one morning attending a press conference for an up and coming Australian movie. When the press conference was over I walked outside and to my amazement saw Robert Wagner standing out the front of the hotel in a bathrobe. I walked up to him and asked for a photo with him. He was happy to do that for me. He then was rushed off to the movie set, which was across the road from the hotel. A few minutes later I got a photo with Stephanie, who was also in a bathrobe.

Robin Williams 1996

Robin came out to Sydney in 1996 to promote the movie *The Birdcage*. I knew that he was in Sydney as there was a photo of him in the paper but I didn't know where he was staying. So on this particular day I headed into the city because I had to take some photos of the city for an assignment that I was doing as part of a photography course.

This was definitely my lucky day. As I was setting up my camera my friend told me that Robin Williams was walking in our direction. I looked up and there he was. He had a backpack on and was just like any other tourist taking in the sights of Sydney. As he walked passed us I asked Robin for a photo with him. He happily posed for the photo and off he went walking around Sydney taking his own photos. Now how lucky was that.

Roger Moore 1996

Roger visited Sydney in 1996 as a goodwill ambassador for UNICEF. He took over the role as celebrity ambassador when Audrey Hepburn died in 1992. Roger is my favourite James Bond so it was a great thrill for me to meet 007. He did a very relaxed press conference in the bar of a Sydney hotel and afterwards hung out with a few of the media that were lingering.

I told him that the year before I had met Pierce Brosnan and that when I got a photo with Pierce he used his finger as a gun in the photo. Roger thought that was a great idea but told me to pretend to shoot him so I could tell people that I not only was shot by a Bond but I also shot one as well. What a great guy.

Sting 1996

I have met Sting a few times over the years and he is always very good to the fans. On this occasion in 1996 Sting was in Sydney to perform some concerts. A friend of mine desperately wanted to meet him and asked if I was trying to photograph him again. I told her that I had got him a few years before and that I didn't need to again. So I left it up to her to find out where he was staying.

My friend rang me the next day to say that she had rang about ten hotels in Sydney but she couldn't find where he was staying. 'What name are you asking for?' I asked. My friend replied, 'Mr. S Ting'. This was one of the funniest things I had ever heard. I then did some investigating and found the hotel where Sting, not Mr. S. Ting was staying and we met him after one of his shows.

Sylvester Stallone 1996

Stallone came out to Sydney in 1996 for the opening of the Planet Hollywood restaurant. In 1996 Sly was one of the biggest stars in the world and he was, to say the very least, extremely hard to meet. While most international celebrities stayed at one hotel, Stallone stayed at another hotel away from all of the media and fans that the other hotel attracted. I tried twice for him at his hotel but I couldn't get anywhere near him. He had his own security team with him from the States and they were good.

On the opening night of Planet Hollywood all of the stars had a huge party at a five star hotel. Stallone was the last to arrive and was rushed into the party. My friend and I were determined to meet him, so we sat in my car and waited across the road for the party to finish. One by one the fans and media started to leave until eventually my friend and I were the only two left. As the night went on my friend and I fell asleep in my car.

I awoke to the sound of voices; it was Stallone and his security team just standing on the side of the road. My friend and I calmly walked over to Stallone and asked him if we could have our photo with him. He said, 'You guys are crazy,' gave us a smile and put his arm in the air to signal for us to stand next to him for the photos. We were crazy—after the photo I looked at my watch, it was 3.30am. We were very lucky that night as we found out that his limousine driver didn't have the car ready for him and he was waiting for it to arrive. That's why he was waiting on the side of the road. Mission accomplished!

Tina Turner 1996

Tina Turner is definitely one of the hardest celebrities that I have ever met to get an autograph or a photo from. I have met her a few times over the years and have always found her to be very difficult. In fact in the early 1990s when I met her she told me to leave a rare record that I had at the front desk of her hotel, telling me that she would sign it for me later that day. When I went back the following day to pick up my very rare record, the hotel's staff told me that there was no item at the front desk, and it never turned up. This was a good lesson for me and I have never made that mistake again.

In 1996 I went to her press conference and afterwards I asked her to sign a Mad Max poster for me. She didn't want to but her manager told her that she should sign it as they didn't want any bad press. She turned down my request for a photo with me but luckily a photographer friend of mine snapped this photo of her signing my poster.

Tom Cruise and Nicole Kidman 1996

Long before Brad and Ange there was Tom and Nicole. During their marriage in the 1990s Tom and Nicole were the most famous couple in the world. They were also the hardest celebrities to meet. In 1990 Tom and Nicole visited Sydney on a holiday. They had not married yet so their relationship was a huge story for the world's media. Because Nicole is Australian their every move was constantly documented by the Australian press.

On one of their days in Sydney my friend and I waited for them to arrive back at their hotel. The media were waiting out the front of the hotel and the local shopkeeper told me that Tom and Nicole had been leaving through the back. So my friend and I waited out the back of the hotel. When they arrived in the back lane in Tom's rented Porsche my friend and I held up a sign saying: 'Tom and Nicole, we just want an autograph. We are fans.'

Tom stopped his car and with his trademark smile waved us over to the driver's seat of the car. When we walked over to the side of the car he quickly accelerated and drove straight past us. This gives you a small insight into how difficult they were to meet.

In 1996 Tom and Nicole were in town for their usual Christmas break. I received a phone call from a friend telling me that they were at Jane Campion's house, so I thought I would drive past to have a look. When I got to the house there were a few photographers waiting down the street. When the couple left the house my friend and I asked them if we could have a photo taken with them. Tom said that if it was okay with Nicole he would also do it. Lucky for us Nicole agreed to pose and we ended up with a great photo in between one of the most famous couples (at that time) in the world.

Tony Hawk 1996

When I was a kid in the 1980s skateboard rider extraordinaire Tony Hawk was my idol. I had a Tony Hawk skateboard, T-shirt, shorts, stickers and anything else with his name on it. I liked him so much that I rang the company in Santa Barbara in the US to ask if Tony Hawk was going to come out to Australia to do some exhibition skating. The lady that I spoke to must have felt sorry for me because she sent me a Tony Hawk pack that included a signed postcard.

So in 1996 when I heard that Tony was going to be performing down at Sydney's Bondi Beach I was down there early. About an hour before the show was to start a hired van pulled up in the car park at the beach and out climbed Tony; he was by himself and I couldn't have been happier. I went up to him and had a photo taken with him sitting in the back of his car. After the skating exhibition Tony went across the road to a surf shop and signed autographs for about 200 people. And yes I still have my signed postcard from 1988. How cool.

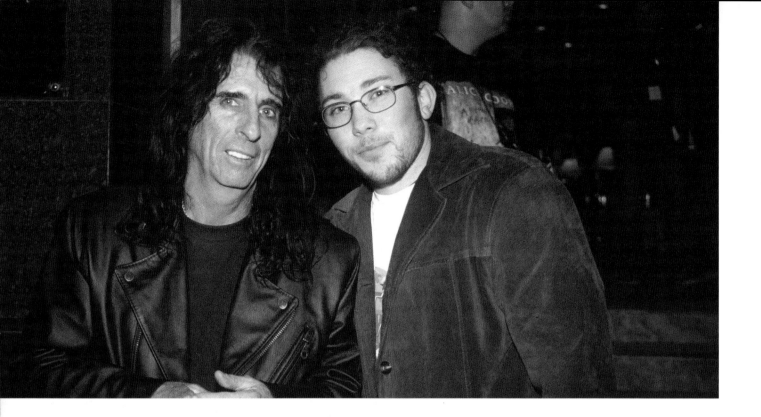

Alice Cooper 1997

I first met Alice in 1990 when he was doing a press conference to promote his Trash world tour. In 1990 I was a 16-year-old kid and I just walked into the press conference. The photo that I had taken with him in 1990 was blurry so when he came back out to Sydney seven years later I met him again to update my photo. Alice was really nice and very quiet, but I can't say the same about his security guard—the guy in the background of this photo.

When Alice got out of his car and walked over to me his security guard told me to get back and that Alice wasn't going to do anything. Now I was very calm and I couldn't get back anymore as I was actually leaning against the wall of the hotel. Alice told the guy that it was okay for me to get a photo with him. During the time I was with Alice the security guard kept looking up and down the road for any other Alice Cooper fans about to jump out of the bushes.

I was telling Alice that I went to his show in 1990 and how much I had enjoyed it when the security guard spotted a few people walking towards the hotel, and mid conversation told Alice that he had to get into the hotel as there were a bunch of fans heading in their direction. Alice went into the hotel; the apparent Alice Cooper fans turned out to be Alice's band walking back from a bar up the road!

Chris Cornell 1997

Now in this photo of me and Soundgarden musician Chris doesn't it looks like I'm desperately leaning over to get into the photo? Well, I am. After their first gig in Sydney I waited with a few other Soundgarden fans for the band to arrive back at their hotel. In the mid 1990s Soundgarden, Pearl Jam and Nirvana were the three biggest bands in the world, due to their sound which was to be known as Grunge.

When the lead singer Chris came back to the hotel the fans rushed at him and one particular fan who was very small wouldn't let go of him. So I had to lean over her to get the photo with him. After Soundgarden broke up Chris joined the band Audioslave, which was formed with three members from Rage Against The Machine.

Claudia Schiffer 1997

Claudia was one of the supermodels in the 1990s and during that period was one of the most famous people in the world. The media and her adoring public followed her every move. So when she came to Sydney in 1997 to promote her workout video, there was a lot of security to protect her.

After her press conference Claudia was escorted out of a staff door at the hotel. I would never had known this, if I hadn't noticed the three security guards who were standing very nervously out the front of the door. So I joined them. When Claudia came out of the door the security guards tried to block me from asking her for a photo, but she heard me asking and stopped for this photo. My friend and I joked that if and when we got the photo with her we were going to try to put on our 'modelling poses' for the photo. I think I ended up looking more scared than anything else.

Gene Simmons 1997

In 1997 Gene, Paul, Ace and Chris made the trip down under as the original KISS for the very first time. When they arrived they did a press conference to promote their gigs. As the days went on, about twenty other KISS fans and I waited for them at their hotel and airport. On the day that they were leaving Sydney about 30 fans turned up at the airport to get their final autographs and photos and for this girl a kiss from Gene. Now I shouldn't point this out, but isn't that a wedding ring on her finger? Oops, let's hope the hubby is a KISS fan as well.

Gregory Peck 1997

In 1996 I had read that Gregory Peck was in Melbourne to do the television movie *Moby Dick*. So my friend and I drove twelve hours down to Melbourne from Sydney and straight to the movie set, which was situated on an air force base. We sat in the car park, which was also a car park for an aeroplane museum; we obviously couldn't get anywhere near the movie set. We didn't know where he was staying so we just sat in the car park hoping to see something that would lead us to the great man.

After a few nervous hours of waiting, a car pulled up next to us. To our total surprise it was Mr Peck, who wanted to have a look at the aeroplane museum because he was a fighter pilot in World War II. We both jumped out of the car and introduced ourselves. Mr Peck did not disappoint us; he was a true gentleman and could not believe that we had driven from Sydney just to meet him.

After a few photographs and general conversation, I asked Mr Peck if he would sign an original movie poster for *To Kill A Mockingbird*. Mr Peck signed the poster and as he was just about to hand it back to me he noticed that it said on the poster 'Not Suitable For Children'. He looked at the poster again and said that it was ridiculous that it would say this on the poster as there were children in the entire movie.

Harry Connick Jr 1997

In 1993 musician Harry Connick Jr was making a name for himself as a modern day crooner. He toured Australia around this time and I went along to see one of his shows. After the concert I met him back at his hotel but I found him to be a little stuck up. He wouldn't pose for a photo and would only sign one autograph, even though I had my mum with me who also wanted one.

Fast forward a few years to 1997 and Harry toured Australia again. After his first show in Sydney I went down to his hotel and waited for him to arrive. He went straight into the bar and started to play the piano. I got a free mini concert.

After about twenty minutes on the piano I casually went up to him and asked for a photo with him. This time he was fantastic and he was in a really friendly mood. The strange thing was that no-one else recognised him and all of the people in the bar that night still have no idea that Harry Connick Jr was playing for them.

Jon Bon Jovi 1997

In 1989 I tried desperately to meet musician Jon Bon Jovi. The only problem was that so did 100 other Bon Jovi fans. In 1993 Bon Jovi toured Australia and I was lucky enough to have my photo taken with Jon but unfortunately I lost the roll of film. In 1997 Bon Jovi came back to Sydney for a few concerts. I had spent a day or so waiting for the band, Jon especially, at their hotel but his security were taking him in and out of the hotel via the basement.

One night after their concert my friend and I waited in the hotel bar because we had heard over the years that the band members usually have a drink in the bar after their shows. At around 1am, Jon came into the bar with his security guard and sat down for a drink. My friend and I had to play it cool so we patiently waited for Jon to finish his drink and as he was walking past us to leave the bar we pretended that we had just noticed him and asked for a photo with him. His security guard said no, but because there were only two of us Jon said that he would do the photo.

Kevin Spacey 1997

In 1997 I had never heard of actor Kevin Spacey. But it was just before he made it big in Hollywood. My friend was a huge fan of a movie that Kevin appeared in called *The Usual Suspects,* so I reluctantly went down to the hotel to wait for him. Kevin came back to the hotel from dinner one night and we met him as he was entering the hotel. He was very quiet and slightly shy, but he was kind enough to give each of us a photo.

I read recently that Kevin was doing a play in London and after the play he would sign autographs for the waiting fans but he would not do photos. I guess I was lucky I got him when I did.

KISS 1997

I received a phone call the day that KISS were to have their press conference in Sydney to promote their Australian tour. This was the very first time that all four original band members had toured Australia. When I got to the press conference, the other photographers and I were told to go to the front of the stage and wait for the band to arrive. When they did I wasn't happy with the angle that I was getting so I left where I was and approached a balcony area. As I got to the balcony I was confronted by a security guard who told me that I wasn't allowed up to the balcony as it was for staff only. I then told him that I was the official photographer and that I needed to take a few photos of the band from that angle. The trick worked and I ended up with some great photos of Gene, Ace, Peter and Paul.

Kylie Minogue 1997

Now this is a photo! Kylie Minogue giving yours truly a kiss on the cheek. By 1997 I had about twenty photos with Kylie so I thought that I needed something a little different. I went to the airport one day when she was flying out of Sydney and showed her a bunch of photos of me and her. Kylie couldn't get over how different we both looked over the years. I said to her that I wanted something different for the next photo. She said to my friend who was going to take the photo, 'I've got an idea. Are you ready to take it?' My friend was. Kylie then put her arms around me and gave me a kiss on the cheek. It was all over in about three seconds but I was wishing that the camera was playing up and that we had to hold this pose for a little longer. I guess a three second kiss from Kylie Minogue is nothing to complain about.

Mike Myers 1997

Funny guy Mike Myers came to Sydney in 1997 to promote his movie *Austin Powers International Man Of Mystery*. I went down to the hotel that he was staying at and waited for him to come in or out. Not too long after I got to the hotel a black stretch limousine pulled up out the front and out got Mike. He was in casual tracksuit pants and had a plastic bag with him that had food in it. He looked more like a backpacker than a Hollywood star. The face that he is pulling in the photo with him is a similar expression to the ones that he does in his *Wayne's World* movies.

Mike Patton 1997

In late 1989 Mike Patton's band Faith No More came out to Sydney for a few small gigs and to promote their new album. I met them at their hotel with about 15 other fans but didn't have a camera with me so I missed out on a photo with Mike with his long hair.

In 1997 Mike was in Sydney for a few gigs and I literally bumped into him in the lobby of a hotel. I was actually waiting for Jon Bon Jovi, who I shot just moments before seeing Mike. I like this photo as it shows Mike holding a suit jacket and a bottle of beer in the same hand. A stylish rocker in the making.

Oliver Stone 1997

Director Oliver Stone came to Sydney in 1997 to promote his movie *U Turn*. My friend and I went down to the hotel he was staying at and waited all day for him to come out. Now when I say all day I really mean all day. We got to the hotel at about 10am and during the day we kept seeing Oliver walk past the front doors of the hotel but he wouldn't come out to meet us. After you wait a certain amount of time you think to yourself, well, I've waited this amount of time I should wait a bit longer until we get the shot. So we stood out the front of his hotel until the evening.

At 8pm we noticed that Oliver had walked out the back door of the hotel, so we went around the back and asked him for a photo. He didn't really want to do it, so I told him that we had been waiting all day for him. He said that he'd seen me and my friend waiting for him and that he didn't care. I then asked him again for the photo, to which he agreed, but when I got the film processed Oliver had his eyes closed in my photo, and in my friend's photo he turned his head just as I took it. There's no need to be rude!

Rowan Atkinson 1997

Mr Bean, or should I say Rowan Atkinson, came to Sydney in 1997 to promote his movie *Mr Bean*.
I met him at a press conference that he did to promote the movie. The entire time that he was at the press conference and the movie premiere he stayed in the character of Mr Bean. After the press conference Rowan posed for the media with the Sydney Opera House in the background. After the photographers had finished I asked Rowan if I could have my photo with him. He said it was fine and gave me this photo.

Out of all of my photos that I have with almost 1000 celebrities this photo gets the best response from people because he is pulling his Mr Bean face. It's a funny photo with a very funny guy.

Silverchair 1997

I accidentally met Australian band Silverchair in January 1997 when I was at the airport waiting for Soundgarden to arrive. Now, a group shot with a band is very hard to achieve because obviously you have to get all of the members of the band together at the same time. Luckily for me they were still quite young and travelled as a group.

They were very shy and quiet and just seemed to be a bit uncomfortable at the attention that I had brought to them. After I got the group photo a few other fans recognised them and had photos taken with them. I'll give them credit: they gave everyone who asked a group photo, which they didn't have to do.

Fast forward a few years to 2005 and I met the lead singer of Silverchair Daniel Johns at a charity gig that he was doing at the Sydney Opera House. I asked him if I could get a photo with him but he turned down my request telling me that every time he posed for a photo part of his soul died. Now that's an interesting one.

Sir Peter Ustinov 1997

In 1997 Sir Peter came to Sydney with a film crew to do a television series about Aboriginal performers. On this particular night Ustinov and his film crew were filming an Aboriginal performer at an outer city pub. When I arrived at the pub Ustinov was sitting on an old lounge chair surrounded by a group of rowdy 20-something-year-olds who had obviously had a few too many drinks The packed pub was grotty and most of the patrons didn't really know who Ustinov was, but they had an idea that he was someone famous.

After his filming obligations were over Ustinov went out the front of the pub and waited for his car to pick him up. I took this photo of him just as his car was coming down the street. It's one of my favourite photos of a celebrity because of the incongruity; a legend dressed like a proper gentleman, holding his walking stick, standing outside a pub, next to a bus stop with faded graffiti behind him. I just love the realism of the photo.

Michael Hutchence 1989-1997

The first real celebrity photo I ever took was of INXS in late 1989. Over the next couple of days after I took this shot, I went down to the Sydney Opera House and waited for the guys to finish rehearsals. Each day I was fortunate enough to meet Michael, Garry, Kirk Jon, Tim and Andrew. They were all, and still are, extremely friendly, down to earth and very generous with their time. Sadly (for me) the week passed and so had their time at the Opera House.

I found out a few days later that Michael Hutchence was staying at the Sebel Townhouse Hotel. The following weekend I went to the hotel to see if I could meet him again. After a day of waiting I heard the roar of Michael's Harley Davidson motorcycle coming down the street. Michael drove his Harley into the car park of the hotel. I was so excited to see him that I ran down into the car park. The doorman at the hotel saw me running and gave chase. After a few seconds I ended up standing next to Michael and waited for him to take his helmet off. The doorman, who was trying to protect his celebrity guest from a 16-year-old school kid, ran down to the car park and ordered me back onto the street. Michael gave me a warm smile and told the over enthusiastic doorman that I was okay.

I spoke to Michael for a few minutes and soon realised that I had never met anyone quite like him. I was only 16 at the time and had no idea what charisma meant, but I knew that Michael was very special.

I found out from my meeting with Michael that INXS were recording a new album at Rhinoceros Recording Studios in Surry Hills (Sydney). In January 1990 I went to 'Rhinos' to see if I could meet INXS again. I stood out the front of the studio for a few hours, but couldn't see any members from INXS. Just as I was about to leave I saw Tim Farriss drive into the car park. I waited for him to walk out and asked him if any of the other members had arrived.

Tim was in total shock that I was waiting for him and the other guys, as he had parked his car in Rhinos just to do some shopping in nearby Oxford Street and was not there to do any recording. Tim told me that I was about two weeks too early and I should come back later in the month.

Two weeks passed and I went back to Rhinos, this time with a bit more luck. I waited outside the studio and after only 30 minutes I heard Michael's Harley Davidson roaring down the street. He parked his Harley on the footpath and I walked over to him and said hello, to which he replied 'Hello, mate, how are you?' We chatted and he was very kind and down to earth. Over the next couple of hours the other guys arrived and greeted me with friendly smiles and had time for a chat.

I enjoyed my day at Rhinos so much that I went back the next day and the next day again. I soon found myself spending more time at Rhinos than at school. In late January of 1990 I left school and became a full-time pupil at Rhinos where my teachers were Michael, Kirk, Garry, Tim, Jon and Andrew. Hours turned into days, days turned into weeks and weeks turned into months—I was hanging out with INXS on a daily basis. I had bought a $90 camera earlier in the year and began to take photos of my favourite band.

I was a 16-year-old kid and INXS were the greatest guys in the world to hang around. They would always pose for a photo, have a chat with me and if there were any parties inside the studio I was always invited. One night when I was at Rhinos Michael came out to the foyer and invited me and two friends who were waiting with me into the studio for a listening party.

I found myself sitting on a black leather lounge with Michael Hutchence sitting next to me singing the song 'Bitter Tears'. This was a night that I will never forget!

Eventually I was waiting at Rhinos fifteen hours a day, five days a week! Most days I would just sit in the foyer of the studios by myself until my friends finished work and school. They would often join me for the 'evening shift'.

As the years passed I continued to hang-out with INXS and decided that, due to my collection of photographs of INXS and in particular Michael, I wanted to become a photographer.

One day in 1992 I was having a conversation with Michael and I told him that I wanted to become a photographer. Michael told me that he would help me. So from that day on I began to practise taking photos of him. He would always pose for my camera and if I had an idea for a photo Michael would go out of his way to help me.

I spent every moment I possibly could following INXS around, but mainly focused on Michael. He is the most charismatic person that I have ever met! People ask me almost on a daily basis what he was like. And to tell you the truth, words cannot describe him. When Kylie Minogue was on Michael Parkinson's television show a few years ago he asked her, 'What was Michael Hutchence like? Kylie answered, 'Did you ever meet Michael'? He hadn't and Kylie went on to tell him that unless you met Michael you couldn't really describe him. That quote from Kylie is so true. How do you describe the most charismatic person that you have ever met to someone who never had the pleasure of meeting him? You simply can't.

In 1990 I was able to spend more and more time with INXS. If there were any listening parties inside the studios my friends and I would sit outside the foyer of the studios and hope that someone would invite us in. Usually just as the party was getting under way Michael would come sliding out of the studio and with a cheeky grin stand at the front door and simply say, 'Are you guys coming in?' Michael and the other guys would have known how much this would have meant to me and my two friends.

I have to say with all sincerity that the band could not have been any nicer. They never said no to any of my requests and were always extremely generous with their time. In fact I caught up with Andrew, Jon, Tim, Garry and Kirk in late 2006 and they treated me like a long lost friend.

For the next seven years, I followed INXS around from the rehearsal studios to the recording studios, to hotels, airports and backstage. If they were there so was I and I always had my camera with me. Over the years I got to know Michael better than the other band members. I was fortunate to spend time with him every time he visited Sydney, which was at least once a year.

In 1992 I was at the ABC TV station at Gore Hill where the guys were rehearsing for an upcoming tour. Rehearsals had finished for the night and Michael asked if I needed a lift back over the Sydney Harbour Bridge. Of course I said yes (even though my mum was waiting down the road in her car!) and this happened five nights. One night he asked me if I remembered the film clip for 'Just Keep Walking'. I told him that I did, and he said that INXS had filmed it just nearby and he would drive me down to show me. When we got down to the warehouse, the gates were locked the warehouse so unfortunately we couldn't go in to have a look. As we were driving over the Sydney Harbour Bridge a Doors song came on the radio. At first Michael started to sing softly. I asked him if he liked The Doors. 'Yeah they're fucking great!' he said. He turned up the radio and started singing. I sat next to him thinking, my God, I am hearing Jim Morrison and Michael Hutchence sing a song together.

Over the years Michael continued to help me with my photography. In early 1994, he even sat for a photo shoot for over an hour. He once told me that I had the best photo collection of him in the world. This was an exceptionally generous thing for him to say to me considering all the great photographers who had photographed him over the years. The very last photo of Michael alive was with me, taken by his dad, Kelland Hutchence, just two days prior to his untimely death.

I was just a 16-year-old school kid when I first met Michael. I wasn't anyone famous, my parents weren't movie stars or rock stars. I was just a fan and Michael took me under his wing and helped me to realise my dream. He didn't have bodyguards, he didn't have an ego. I saw him sit in pubs and have a beer with everyone else. I saw him get on a ferry on Australia Day in 1992 and sit outside with (then girlfriend) Helena Christensen and happily chat with the rest of the passengers and sign autographs for a ferryload of overexcited girls!

On Saturday 22 November 1997 I went to the Ritz Carlton hotel in Double Bay to pick Michael up and take him to ABC studios for rehearsals. Michael had told me on the Thursday that he was going to leave between 10.30am and 11am. I arrived at the hotel at approximately 9.30am as I did not want to miss the opportunity of driving Michael. Just after 12pm a few security guards walked outside the hotel and waited near the loading dock. A few moments passed and an ambulance arrived and drove into the loading dock. Three or four security guards from the hotel escorted the ambulance inside.

Soon after the ambulance arrived a police vehicle turned up. About 45 minutes had passed since the police arrived and I was beginning to become slightly nervous. There was no sign of Michael, instead there were police and ambulance officers. A few minutes passed and I saw a man running towards the hotel with a news camera on his shoulders. The man ran up to me and asked 'What's going on?' I told him that I didn't know and asked him if he knew. He then told me that he was sitting up the road in his news vehicle listening to the police radio and had heard that an Australian international rock star had been found dead in one of the hotel rooms. He then asked me if I knew who it could be.

I knew then that it was Michael, but I told him that I didn't know. The first thing I did was ring my girlfriend at work. When she answered the phone I said to her, 'I think Michael is dead.' My girlfriend told me later that as soon as I said those words, the whole department store where she was working went completely black.

When I think of Michael, I smile. He was Australia's first and only international rock star. He was and still is my idol. I have honestly never met anyone else like him, famous or non-famous. Women wanted to be with him and guys wanted to be just like him.

It was because of INXS and Michael that I decided to become a photographer. In 2005 my first book was released, *Australian Legends: People whose story we should know*. My life has been shaped in a unique way because of my involvement with Michael Hutchence. He has inspired me throughout my whole life.

Michael Hutchence
wearing yellow shirt in kitchen
1990

Michael took my friend and me on a tour of Rhinos recording studios late one night. Once inside the doors he walked us through the reception, down the hallway and into the kitchen. He told us that we could make ourselves at home then extended his arms and said, 'This is the famous Rhinos kitchen.' I asked him for a photo. As always, he obliged (Michael never said no to my photo requests). Michael then made us coffees, opened up a pack of biscuits and took us into the recording studio for a private tour.

Michael riding his push bike in the streets of Surry Hills, Sydney
1990

Michael used to ride his push bike every couple of days when he had a spare few hours off from recording. He used to give me his bike once he had finished and I would go on rides around Sydney. I thought I was so cool to be riding Michael's bike. In this photo Michael paused so I could snap him in 'slow motion'.

Michael Hutchence and Kylie Minogue 1990

When Michael and Kylie were dating in 1990 they were one of the hottest couples in the world. This particular year shaped Kylie's life both personally and professionally. They used to live in The Connaught apartment building in Sydney. I went to the motor show one particular weekend and when I was walking through the city to catch the bus I noticed Michael and Kylie walking through Hyde Park and back to their apartment. As they crossed the road Michael saw me and waved me over. He introduced me to Kylie and I got this photo. It captures both superstars on a rare day off. Kylie looks so young and innocent.

Michael Hutchence, Rob Lowe and INXS Drummer Jon Farriss 1990

One night when I was waiting for INXS at Rhinoceros Recording Studio, Hollywood actor Rob Lowe turned up to hang out with the band. When they left the studios I got this photo with the three of them. In later years this photo granted me access to Rob Lowe while he was at the races in a VIP area in Sydney. He told me that they all went to Kings Cross (Sydney's red light district) and he got so drunk that he woke up with a tattoo.

It's such a cool photo; I'm just a 16-year-old kid who was losing it just to be in the photo and the other three are just playing it cool.

Michael Hutchence
and
Helena Christensen 1994

Michael was in Sydney to do some shows with INXS in 1994. Little did anyone know that it would be his last tour of Australia with INXS. I had this photo taken with Michael and his then girlfriend Helena Christensen as they were about to fly out of Sydney for the final part of the tour.

Michael Hutchence 1997

Michael was in Sydney in early 1997 for rehearsals with INXS. I rang Michael's dad, Kell, and he told me where Michael was staying. I met Michael at his hotel and he said that he and some friends were going to a café in Sydney's red light district in Kings Cross. I met Michael at the café and when he saw me he gave me a big hug and told me how good it was that I turned up. This is my favourite photo with Michael.

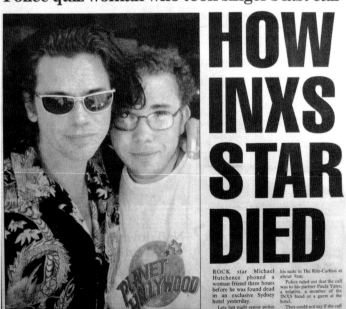

Michael Hutchence 1997

On 20 November 1997 I went down to the Ritz Carlton Hotel in Double Bay to catch up with Michael. As I arrived I saw Michael and his dad Kell walk out of the hotel and go across the road to another hotel for a bite to eat. I walked on over and said hello to both of them. We all had a chat for a while and Michael told me that his partner Paula Yates was going to be in Sydney the following Wednesday and I should get a photo with them both. He was in a quiet and shy mood but was very relaxed and chatted with me about the upcoming tour. He also asked me if I could get him a copy of a 1989 *Rolling Stone* magazine that he was on the cover of. After the chat Kell took this photo of me and Michael. Within 48 hours of this photo being taken Michael Hutchence was dead.

The morning after Michael died this photo appeared on the front cover of numerous newspapers. I still have people coming up to me today who just want to talk about Michael. He touched so many people's lives from all around the world.

Adam Sandler 1998

Funny guy Adam Sandler visited Sydney with Drew Barrymore in 1997 to promote their movie *The Wedding Singer*. Both Drew and Adam have a strong fan base so when I went down to the hotel to meet him there were about 20 fans waiting for them. The first few days Adam was doing mostly media but once that was over he went for a walk and stopped for all of the fans. Apparently he's cross -eyed and doesn't like looking straight down the lens in photos—lucky for me he's wearing his sunglasses.

Baz Luhrmann 1998

In 1998 I went down to where the Sydney to Hobart Yacht Race starts in Rushcutters Bay. I go down every year just to have a look and photograph the multimillion dollar yachts and to see if I can spot any wandering celebrities. On this particular occasion director/writer Baz Luhrmann was sailing with Lachlan Murdoch. By sheer coincidence I was wearing the same shirt as their official team shirt. As I was about to take this photo of Baz, he held up a packet of travel sickness tablets. It made for a funny photo.

Billy Connolly 1998

On this particular day in 1998 I was walking around the foreshore of Sydney Harbour just taking some stock photos for the photo agency that I was working for, when I noticed comedian Billy taking a walk as well. I had to look twice at him as at first glance I wasn't 100 per cent sure if it was him. He didn't really look like the Billy Connolly we're used to seeing on television but I guess that was part of his plan.

I walked up to him and asked if I could take a photo of him. He happily agreed and then spent a few minutes having a chat with me. He told me that because his wife Pamela Stevenson is an Australian they usually spend every Christmas in Australia to escape the UK cold. You can tell in this photo that it was very hot on this particular day.

Drew Barrymore 1998

Drew came out to Sydney in 1998 to promote *The Wedding Singer* with co-star Adam Sandler. Both Adam and Drew have a type of cult following with fans, so when they arrived in town out came all of the fans. After a few days of both stars doing media, they both went for a walk out the back of the hotel. Even though there were about 20 fans, both stars were extremely friendly and signed and posed for photos.

Drew was very cute and took photos of her fans with her camera. It's one of those cameras that prints out the photo as soon as you take it; let's hope she's got a digital camera now.

Jerry Seinfeld 1998

The day after the hit television show *Seinfeld* aired
for the very last time in the US in 1998, its star Jerry
Seinfeld came straight to Sydney for a week of stand-up
shows. Jerry was very accessible. The only problem was
that he wouldn't sign autographs and if you wanted a
photo with him you had to walk next to him without
touching him while someone took the photo.

This photo of Jerry and me was taken when he and
his three bodyguards went for a walk around Bondi
Beach. He didn't say a word to anyone, instead his
security team told the public what they could and
couldn't do. It was very amusing as Bondi Beach was
packed on this day, so a lot of people were just walking
up to Jerry as he strolled around. Every time
someone went up to say hi or to shake his
hand his security would tell people not to
touch him, but if they wanted they could
get a photo walking next to him. Jerry
didn't have to stop for fans but the fans
still got a photo walking next to him—
a win–win situation.

141

Kylie Minogue 1998

During the mid to late 1990s Kylie's career had slowed down. In 1998 Kylie played a string of sell-out intimate concerts for her dedicated fans. My girlfriend and I have been Kylie fans since the late 1980s so we went to two of her shows, both of which were brilliant. At the end of the show silver glitter fell from above as part of the show. I knew that this was the final song because I'd been the night before.

Just after the glitter had fallen I went down to the side of the stage to try to get some photos, and by sheer luck Kylie noticed me and gave me a smile. I quickly put the camera up to my eye and snapped this photo. It was so quick that I didn't even have time to notice if the camera was on the correct settings. Luckily it was. This photo is my favourite concert photo ever.

Rob Thomas 2004

Rob Thomas 1998

I bumped into musician Rob Thomas one night at the Sebel Townhouse Hotel after a night out watching a friend's band play a pub gig in a nearby hotel. As my friend and I were walking back to our car we noticed the front man of Match Box 20 sitting by himself in the foyer of the hotel. My friend and I went in and each had a photo taken with him.

In later years during interviews he tells the story that due to him drinking too much beer while in Australia in 1998 he put on a bit of unwanted weight. All I'm saying is that when I met him again in LA in 2004 he looked liked a completely different person. It's amazing what a few beers in Australia can do to a rock star.

Serena and Venus Williams 1998

In January 1998 Serena and Venus were in Sydney to play a tennis tournament in preparation for the Australian Open. I went to have a look at the hotel where the players stay every year and noticed a young Venus and Serena just hanging out in the lobby. This was just before they broke onto the world's tennis stage and dominated the game for a number of years.

   Until I looked at this photo recently I had forgotten that they used to have beaded braids in their hair. They were both very shy and a bit embarrassed that I asked them for this photo. They were giggling during the photo. I don't know how tough it would be today to get the photo in between them. I'm so glad I met them when I did.

Bono 1998

Bono is by far one of the nicest celebrities I have ever met. U2 is my second favourite band and I have met them in 1989, 1993, 1998 and 2006. Bono comes out of his hotel every day and spends time with the fans. In 1998 there were about 40 fans outside his hotel. His security came out and told us that Bono was coming out to meet with us. He got us to all wait in a single line and about ten minutes later Bono came out, signed autographs and had his photo taken with every fan. He really loves his fans.

Some nights after concerts he sits outside the hotel with the fans and just hangs out. Considering he is the biggest rock star in the world this is quite amazing. What you see on television and read in the press is not all for show. He really is a caring and genuine person. What other celebrity of Bono's fame would spend time with their fans every day? And he does this when the media is not around.

A lot of celebrities act 'fan friendly' when the media is around so they look all nice and friendly on television, but once the cameras stop rolling many of them just turn off their charm and forget about the fans. Bono is the complete opposite.

The Edge 1998

The Edge and Bono are the two most popular members of U2. It just so happens that The Edge and Bono are the nicest, therefore the easiest to meet. The Edge is very similar to Bono when it comes to the fans. He always has time for them and if there are too many fans out the front of the hotel, he gets his security to organise them so he can sign and pose for photos.

On this occasion I was lucky enough to meet the The Edge outside a Sydney restaurant, where he not only gave me a photo but signed and gave photos to about 20 other waiting fans.

Sir Anthony Hopkins 1999

It's not everyday that I get to meet someone that I admire. So in 1999 when Sir Anthony came to Sydney to do a few days of filming with Tom Cruise for *Mission Impossible* I had to try to meet him. I found out which hotel he'd been staying at and spoke to a friend of mine who had been trying to meet Anthony with no luck. Apparently Anthony was leaving through the basement of the hotel to avoid the media.

I needed a plan. The media don't usually wait at night for a celebrity because a day time shot is worth much more money. A night photo is usually just a single photo seller. I waited at the hotel one night at about 9pm hoping to catch Anthony coming back from dinner. My plan worked. At 10pm Anthony arrived at the hotel and luckily for me he arrived through the front instead of the basement. I asked him if I could have my photo taken with him and he happily obliged. This really was my lucky night because Anthony must have had a really nice meal and a few drinks as he was a little tipsy.

He asked me to take a photo of him and then asked if I had anything for him to sign. After the photos and signing he told me about his day of filming with Tom Cruise. In fact I probably could have spent as much time with him as I wanted. After a five minute chat I thanked him for his time and he went into the hotel. Sir Anthony is one of my all time favourite actors so meeting him was a huge thrill for me. The next day my friend went back to the hotel to try and meet him and, yep, you guessed it, he left through the basement.

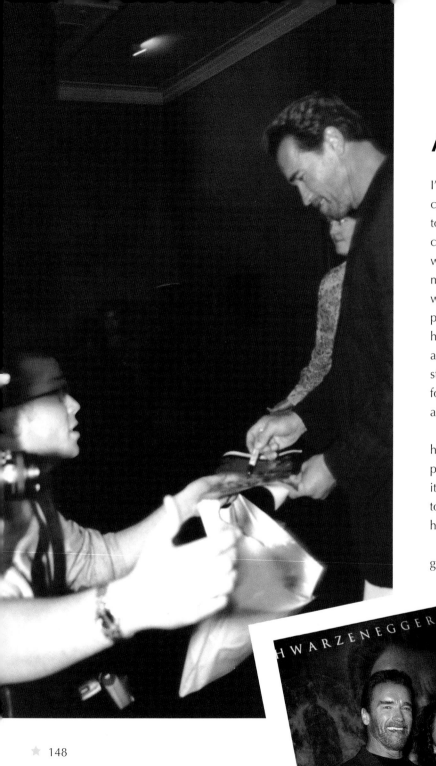

Arnold Schwarzenegger 1999

I'm going to put Arnold into the not-so-friendly celebrity category. Arnold came out to Sydney in 1999 to promote his movie *End Of Days*. He did a press conference with co-star Robin Tunney. Afterwards I went up to the front of the stage and asked him to sign my poster—asking for an autograph stops the celebrity, which then gives you the opportunity to ask for a photo. I pulled out my poster and held it up to him, but he pretended that he didn't see or hear me. There were a bunch of photographers still taking photos so he was standing there with a plastic smile on his face posing for photos. I held the poster up and yelled loudly, asking if he could sign it for me, he still ignored me.

A few photographers caught on to what was happening and they started yelling at him, 'Sign the poster for him, Arnold!' He had no choice but to sign it. As he was signing I was asking him to please look to his left so I could have my photo taken with him but his intermittent hearing problem came back.

Later that night I found out what restaurant he was going to eat at. I arrived after his meal and approached him as he was leaving the restaurant. I asked for an autograph, he wrote an 'A' on the photo then purposely dropped the pen in the gutter. I asked him for a photo to which he replied, 'I don't do photos'. I bent down to get my pen and a cigar was flicked in my direction. Rude. I bet that hearing problem has helped him out in his political career.

Maurice and Barry Gibb 1999

The Bee Gees were back in Sydney in 1999 to work on the production of their musical *Saturday Night Fever*. I had heard that they were going to the casino to watch the rehearsals for the musical. A friend and I went down to the rehearsals and waited for the brothers to leave via the stage door. Robin left first and gave us a photo. A short time later Maurice and Barry left and were kind enough to give us a photo in between them.

Sadly in January 2003 Maurice died of heart complications. A lot of people don't know that the Gibb brothers moved to Australia in the 1960s and spent much of their childhood growing up in Sydney. Their first recordings and shows were all done in Australia.

Ellen DeGeneres 1999

In 1999 I was in the US on a holiday and read one morning that the GLAD Awards were on. On that particular day my girlfriend and I went to the hotel where the awards were to be held and just walked into the lobby. Once in the lobby we noticed a bunch of celebrities just mingling with everyone else. We saw Rosanne Barr, Whoopi Goldberg and comedian Ellen DeGeneres.

I went up to Ellen and asked for a photo; she said yes but added that it had to be quick. My girlfriend snapped the photo and she was off. We then went around and got the other celebrities. If an award ceremony like this was to happen in Sydney there would be no way I could have simply walked around the hotel's lobby and met these celebrities, but in LA these sorts of functions happen every day and night. So usually it's not a big deal.

Today when a B-grade celebrity comes to Sydney it's like a military operation to protect them from maybe one or two fans. I wish the security, PR, hotel workers, and limo drivers would go to LA for a week and see how it works over there.

Ewan McGregor 1999

The first I knew that actor Ewan McGregor was in Sydney in 1999 was when I saw footage of him on television snubbing photographers as he arrived for an opening night of a play. A friend of mine was at the play and tried to get Ewan's autograph but failed. A few weeks passed and I got a phone call from a friend telling me that Ewan was sitting next to him at a restaurant near Kings Cross. I went down to the restaurant and waited about two hours for Ewan to leave. When he did I asked him if I could have a photo and he said, 'Sure you can.' He was in such a great mood; as you can see he was just beaming. In the background of the photo you can see the historic Coke sign which is in Kings Cross.

Because episodes two and three of *Star Wars* were filmed in Sydney I met Ewan a number of times at different events. He was always very friendly and one time in particular signed about 40 autographs for waiting fans.

Heath Ledger 1999

I love to meet minor celebrities; as time passes they turn into major celebrities. This was the case with Heath. It was 1999 and actor Heath Ledger was at the after party at a pub to celebrate the release of the Aussie movie *Two Hands*. Heath had not made it big in Hollywood yet and I got to hang out with him for a few hours. He was just having a fun night with a bunch of friends and he didn't mind that I was taking his photo, he actually enjoyed it.

That same night Russell Crowe turned up to the after party and I sat down and had a beer with him as we spoke about cricketing great Sir Donald Bradman. This was before Russ had made *Gladiator* so even he wasn't a huge star yet. That night Russell was very camera shy and Heath was lapping it up. Now it's the other way around. Russell doesn't mind a photo but Heath hates the media attention.

You can't become Hollywood successful then panic when people start to recognise you and want your photo or autograph. It's really quite simple; if you can't handle fame then don't get into showbiz.

Heath Ledger at the after party for his movie *Two Hands*.

Hugh Hefner 1999

I was in LA in 1999 and a few autograph collectors were nice enough to tell me that Hugh Hefner was attending a party that night at a nightclub. I went to the nightclub and as luck would have it an Aussie was working on the door. I asked him if Hugh was turning up to the club that night and he told me that he was. He then asked me if I wanted to go into the club and wait for Hugh inside. As the conversation continued the guy told me that there was a VIP room for Hugh and his friends and even he couldn't get me into the VIP room. I did the maths and figured that I would have a better chance getting him when he arrived.

After about three hours of waiting, a very long stretch black car pulled up out the front with the number plate Hef 1. About eight girls hopped out of the car and went into the club. About five minutes later another one of these cars pulls up; this time the plates read Hef 2. Another eight girls get out of the car, this time with Hugh. I went up to him and ask if he would sign a *Playboy* for me, but he said he didn't sign *Playboy*s anymore.

He was just about to walk into the club when one of the girls asks me where I was from. 'Australia,' I replied. She then said to Hugh, 'Hugh, this guy is from Australia; go and sign the magazine for him.' Hugh came over and signed the magazine for me. I then explained to him that because I was from Australia I probably wouldn't get another chance to ever meet him again so I asked if I could get a photo with him. The girl who helped me before said to Hugh, 'Give the guy a photo, Hugh. He's from Australia.' Hugh then tells me that it's fine to have a photo with him and my girlfriend quickly snapped it before he went into the club.

The next night I went back to the club to have a chat with the Aussie bouncer and he told me that Hugh was dancing at the club until 7am. Now that's living the *Playboy* lifestyle.

James Caan 1999

In 1999 my girlfriend and I were in the US on a holiday. On this particular day we decided to go to Disneyland; the only problem was that so did everyone else. The week before we went to Disneyland it had been raining quite heavily, so when the rain stopped everyone flocked to the theme park. Once inside we found out that there was a minimum wait of three hours to go on any rides. The place was so full of people it was almost impossible to simply walk around. Amazingly my girlfriend has an eye for spotting celebrities and on this day she somehow spotted actor James Caan.

Now, in 1999 I had heard of James Caan but I had no idea what he looked like. His profile has lifted over the past couple of years because of his starring role in the television series *Las Vegas*. I walked up to James and asked for a photo with him, which he kindly gave me. We then had a chat about Sydney as he had recently been there and he told me that he went to a Sydney Swans football game. After the chat and photo we went our separate ways, but for some strange reason we kept seeing him and his son throughout the day.

I soon noticed that he was going on all of the rides without waiting in the three hour cues because he was a celebrity. You see the guy in the long dark jacket to the left of this photo? He works for Disneyland and he was escorting James and his son around the theme park. When James and his son wanted to go on a ride the Disneyland guy would go to the front of the queue and simply tell the people at the front that a VIP guest was to go on the ride and they had to wait for the next one. I must have seen this happen about five times during the day. In this photo of James and his son, they are on a car ride; after the ride had finished his son wanted to go on it again, so they just stayed on the ride until his son wanted to go to the next ride.

Ah, the power of celebrity. I never feel sorry when celebrities complain about their lives. It is a truly privileged existence.

John McEnroe 1999

John was in Sydney in 1999 to play at a seniors' tennis tournament. I had tried to get a photo with him a few years before with no luck. He wouldn't give me one. After winning a match he arrived back at his hotel and I asked him if I could have a photo with him. He said he didn't do photos or autographs at the hotel and if I wanted one I would have to go to the tennis and he would do it after his match. I took his word for it and the next day I paid $40 for a ticket to watch him play. He won the game and I waited with about five kids for him to leave the court. When he left the court he didn't sign any autographs for the kids and needless to say didn't give me that photo.

So I went straight to his hotel and waited for him to arrive. When he did he went straight for the lifts and didn't look at me. I showed him my $40 ticket for his game and told him that he didn't do anything, even for the kids. He said that I needed to go back the next day to the tennis and he would do it there. I'd believed him once and I knew that he was lying, so I asked him again for the photo.

Then the strangest thing happened. The hotel that he was staying at had about six lifts, and he was agitatedly pressing the buttons for about three minutes but no lifts were opening for him. I just stood my ground and told him that a photo would only take about two seconds and once I got it I would never bother him again. Another 30 seconds passed and still no lifts. Finally he walked over and stood next to me as if to say, take the God damn photo. My girlfriend did and as soon as the photo was taken the lift door opened. He did get me back in some way because as you can see he's not looking at the camera, but this photo with him is better than no photo at all.

Elizabeth Hurley and Hugh Grant 1999

In the mid to late 1990s Liz Hurley and Hugh Grant were one of the hottest couples in the world. So when they visited Sydney in 1999 to promote their movie *Mickey Blue Eyes*, I knew I had to try to get the 'couple photo'. On the day of the movie premiere they left the hotel through the car park so my friend and I couldn't meet them. On their return to the hotel later that night they entered through the front. My friend was a huge Liz Hurley fan and desperately wanted a photo with her.

When they got out of their car my friend and I tried to approach them for a photo but their security would let us get anywhere near them. My friend started to almost beg Elizabeth for the photo. The security were standing in our way so it was up to Elizabeth and Hugh. Hugh was about to walk into the hotel when Elizabeth told the security to let us through to them; my friend's begging worked.

As we got to Elizabeth, Hugh was walking into the hotel so I quickly asked Elizabeth if we could get the photo with both of them. She was kind enough to call Hugh back out for the photo. You can tell by the look on Hugh's face that he wasn't too excited about having his photo taken. The body language is interesting—I'm leaning more towards Elizabeth, but can you blame me? She looked absolutely stunning.

Mark Wahlberg 1999

On my visit to LA in 1999 I had heard that Hugh Hefner was going to be at a nightclub. While I was waiting for Hefner to arrive I noticed a hired car pull up down the street from the club and saw actor Mark Wahlberg and his security guard walking towards the club. Mark waited at the back of the line while the security guy walked up to the fans waiting for celebrities' autographs and told them not to approach Mark for his autograph. His security guard went up to the bouncer at the door and told the guy that Mark Wahlberg was waiting in the line with the everyday people and that he wanted to get him into the club at once.

While this was going on I walked up to Mark and asked him for the photo. He turned around and posed and my girlfriend snapped the photo. His security guard noticed that a photo had been taken, but he didn't see me get the photo so he had no-one to scream at.

Needless to say a few seconds later Mark was taken out of the line and escorted straight into the club to dance the night away with Hugh Hefner, the Playboy girls and the rest of the 'funky bunch'.

Mickey Rooney 1999

When I was a kid my favourite show on television was the *Andy Hardy Series*. Needless to say, Mickey Rooney was one of my all-time favourite actors. In 1994 Mickey toured Australia and I was fortunate to meet him a few times in Sydney. I was told by my friends in America that he wasn't the nicest person to meet—the stories that I had been told portrayed him as a very nasty person. So when I met him in 1994 I was pleasantly surprised to find he was extremely nice and always signed autographs and posed for photos.

Fast forward five years and Mickey was back in Sydney on another concert tour. Because I had met him in 1994 I wasn't going to try for him again but as luck had it a photographer friend shot Mickey and fellow visiting celebrity Arnold Schwarzenegger together in Sydney. My friend phoned me and said that Mickey had called him and had asked for some copies of the photos. My friend couldn't deliver the photos to Mickey's hotel so he asked if I could drop them to his room. I instantly accepted the offer, collected the photos and rang Mickey's room from the hotel reception desk. His wife Jan asked me to come up to their room.

When I got to the room Mickey answered and I gave him the photos. He very rudely snatched them out of my hand and tried to slam the door in my face. I put my foot between the door and the doorframe and told Mickey that he could at least thank me for the photos. He told me to 'F**k' off and tried to close the door. By this stage I had had enough of his rudeness. I opened the door and told him that I had just driven an hour to give him the photos and the least he could do was to sign something for me.

He angrily told me to come into his hotel room, snatched the photo out of my hand, scribbled on it and then threw the photo and pen on the ground. I bent down to collect my things when all of a sudden I felt a nudge to the side of my ribs; Mickey had kneed me! I quickly stood up and was in a state of shock. He was yelling at me to get out of the room, but I stood my ground and told him that I wasn't going until I got a photo with him. His wife heard the noise and rushed out to the hallway of their room. When she saw what was going on she was very embarrassed by her husband's actions. She told Mickey to apologise and to give me a photo as I had delivered the photos that he had asked for. The look on his face is priceless. It was certainly an unusual and almost humorous encounter with a Hollywood legend.

Richard and Mickey 1994

159

Milton Berle 1999

Milton Berle first appeared on television in the US in an experimental broadcast in 1929. Though he wasn't the first person to appear on television he became known as 'Mr Television'.

The Milton Berle Show ran in the US from 1948–1956. The show was so popular that it was responsible for the increase of television sales in the US. My friend met Milton in 1995 at the Fryers Club, a comedians hang-out, in Beverly Hills and told me that Milton went to the club every Wednesday and that he was great to meet.

In 1999 I was in LA and decided that I would try my luck to see if I could meet Milton at the Fryers Club. On a Wednesday afternoon I arrived at the club and was told by the lady at the door that Milton wasn't there on that particular day and she didn't know what day he would be coming. I was convinced that he was inside so I went around the back to the car park and asked one of the attendants if Milton was here. He told me that he couldn't answer that question for me. I then told him that I had come from Australia just to meet Milton, but he was still not giving any information away. I could tell that he felt sorry for me, so I then did something that you see in movies; I gave the guy $20 and asked him if he knew any more information.

As soon as I gave him the $20 he took me over to Milton's black car and told me to wait by the passenger side as Milton was coming out at any moment. About ten minutes later Milton came walking towards his car and the attendant told Milton that I had come from Australia to meet him. Milton was extremely friendly. He signed a few items for me and then posed for some photos with his trademark cigar and smile. To this day it's the best $20 dollars I have ever spent. And they say that money can't buy you happiness.

Neil Diamond 1999

Some celebrities are easy to meet, others are tough. Musician Neil Diamond isn't the toughest to meet but he is one of the toughest if you want a photo with him. I had tried to get a photo with him a few years earlier but he just wouldn't do it; he would sign an autograph but not do the photo.

When he toured Sydney in 1999 I didn't bother to try to meet him. One night I was waiting at a hotel for another visiting celebrity when all of a sudden Neil walked into the foyer of the hotel; he wasn't staying there he was simply visiting his band. (Sometimes the 'star' doesn't stay or travel with the band.) I walked up to him and asked for a photo and to my utter surprise he happily agreed. The funny thing is that if I was waiting for him at his hotel he wouldn't have stopped for a photo but because I bumped into him at a different hotel and he knew that I wasn't waiting for him, he gave me this photo, smile and all.

Evander Holyfield 2000

Boxing champ Evander was in Sydney in 2000 for the Olympic Games. I had no intention of trying to meet him and didn't know where he was staying, but when I went to a hotel in the city to wait for a few of the athletes that were competing at the games, to my surprise Evander was also staying at the hotel. My friend had bought a few boomerangs to give to some of the athletes so when I saw Evander I got my friend to give him one. I took this photo of Evander and his boomerang.

The next day I saw Evander again so I asked him for an autograph. He told me that he was under contract to an autograph/sporting company in the US and he couldn't sign autographs; if I wanted his autograph I could buy one online from the company. Don't these athletes make enough money as it is? Someone like Evander Holyfield, who was the Heavyweight Boxing Champion of the world, makes millions of dollars every time he gets into the ring—so does he really need to make a few extra dollars with his autograph? Signing an autograph is easy and can make someone's day.

Hugh Jackman 2000

I met Aussie actor Hugh Jackman in 2000 when he was back in Sydney for a holiday with his family. I was tipped off about which flight he was going to be on. When he arrived at the international airport he checked his luggage in then went to walk outside. My friend and I approached him for a quick photo. Hugh said that his wife was in the limousine and he was going to drop her off at the domestic terminal, and he would pose for a photo when he got back to the international airport.

I suggested that we do the photo there and then as it would only take a few seconds. Hugh agreed and somewhat embarrassedly posed for a photo or two.

John Frusciante 2000

Red Hot Chili Peppers

This photo proves that rock stars are in a league of their own. In 2000 The Red Hot Chili Peppers toured Australia. I went to the airport to meet them as they were leaving Sydney.

I got a photo with all of the members except for Flea, who rarely does photos. In this photo I'm with guitarist John Frusciante. He told me that he was running late for the flight so he thought that he would bring his breakfast with him to the airport. After this photo he went through security with the bowl, cereal, milk and spoon!

Kylie Minogue 2000

Just another example of how great Kylie is to her fans. Kylie was in Sydney for the 2000 Olympic Games and a friend, who had a broken leg, and I went to her hotel to meet her. Kylie came out of her hotel, walked straight over to us and said 'Hi', then asked my friend how he broke his leg. She asked for a pen and got down on the ground and wrote a message on his cast.

Sir Richard Branson 2000

In 2000 businessman Richard Branson visited Sydney to launch the Virgin mobile phone network. I went to the launch party and Sir Richard was very accessible. After the media did their photos for the night I went up to Sir Richard and asked him to pose with a frisbee. He asked me who I worked for and I replied, 'Like you I work for myself.' I think he liked my answer and he posed with the frisbee.

Russell Crowe 2000

For many years Russell would not give a photo to almost anyone; he was one of the hardest celebrities to get a photo with or even an autograph from. I first met him in 1999 at Heath Ledger's after party for his movie *Two Hands*. I spoke to Russell at the party about cricketing great Sir Donald Bradman and even had a beer with him, but he wouldn't give me a photo with him.

In 2000 Russell came home to Sydney to do a press conference to promote the movie *Gladiator*. After the press conference I quickly got up on stage with him and asked him for a photo. He couldn't refuse as the room was still full of watching media. I handed my friend my camera and I got my first photo with Russell. Over the last couple of years he has become much more relaxed and nine times out of ten will give you a photo and an autograph. In fact the last time I met him in 2005 he joked that I couldn't get a photo with him because I had my lens cap on.

Bill Wyman 2001

For much of 2001 I was based in London. While looking at the local gig guide one day I noticed that ex-Rolling Stones member Bill was to play a pub show near Convent Garden. I went down to the pub after the show and noticed that Bill's car was waiting near the stage door. I walked around to the front of the pub and saw about 30 fans waiting for him to leave. I was by myself and I wanted someone to wait with me at the stage door to take the photo. I approached each fan and told them that they were waiting at the wrong exit, but everyone said I didn't know what I was talking about and that he was going to leave the pub via the front. Eventually I gave up on the fans and waited for Bill by myself.

About two hours later Bill left the stage door and noticed that I was the only fan waiting for him. He happily posed for these two photos, telling me that the stage manager was from New Zealand so because I was from Australia, the New Zealander should take the photo of us. I then asked him to signed a piece of paper for me. I then went around to the front of the pub and yelled out that Bill had just left. One fan asked me to prove it so I showed them all the autograph. In a split second all of them ran around to the back of the pub with cameras, pens, records, posters and guitars to try to meet Bill. Sadly for them Bill was driving off as they got to the stage door. I ended up being the only person that got him that night and I felt bloody great about it.

Michael Caine 2001

Actor Michael Caine was in Sydney in early 2001 for the filming of *The Quiet American*. It was a few days before I was to leave Australia and move to London so I wasn't really thinking about meeting any celebrities, but a friend of mine told me which hotel Michael was staying at and what time he left to go to the set each morning. I thought I would give it a go.

I went down to the hotel at 6am and he left his hotel at 6:15am. He kindly gave me a photo and signed an autograph for me and then told me that he was off to shoot the movie. It was a friendly but quick meeting.

Mohamed Al Fayed 2001

When I was living in London in 2001 I read that Helena Christensen was going to be appearing at Harrods to sign autographs to promote a perfume. I had met Helena a number of times because of my involvement with Michael Hutchence so I thought I would go to Harrods to say hello. After the signing Helena saw me and walked over for a chat. After our chat I approached Harrods owner Al Fayed for a photo with him, but he said that he didn't pose for photos with people unless they were wearing a suit.

I thought that he was joking with me so I approached him again. This time his tone of voice changed. He looked me directly in the eyes and said, 'Listen. I told you before I don't pose with people unless they are wearing a suit.' I told him that I thought that he was joking, to which he replied, 'Does it look like I'm joking with you?' I could hardly believe what he had just said to me. It's one of the strangest excuses that I have ever heard for not wanting to give a fan a photo. I certainly wasn't going to buy a suit from his store.

U2 2001

I was fortunate to get a ticket for my birthday in 2001 to see U2 in London. The show was very emotional as Bono's father had died that very day. I wasn't allowed to take my large camera or lens into the gig so I took these two photos with my instamatic. It was a great show not only because of Bono's emotions but because U2 are simply one of the greatest live bands in the world.

Woody Allen 2001

Comic actor Woody was in London in 2001 and my friend (also Australian) and I desperately wanted to meet him. He had not been to Australia before and it was perhaps our only chance to meet him, so we put on out best suits and went to the Dorchester Hotel and waited inside.

After standing around the lobby for a while we decided to sit down for a drink. After spending £16 on two hot chocolates and waiting three hours, we finally spotted Woody entering the hotel. We got up but were too late—he was in the lift before we were able to meet him.

The next day we thought that we would just wait outside with two other fans. After a day of waiting Woody came back to the hotel in a car and walked over to the other fans. While he was signing autographs for them I told his PR lady that we were from Australia and we simply wanted a photo with Woody. After he signed for the other two fans, Woody went to walk into the hotel, but just before he did the PR lady said, 'Woody, these two guys are from Australia. They just want a photo with you.' Woody turned back around and we got a photo each with him. The funny thing is that we never said a word to him and he never said a word to us. As long as we got the photo…

Bob Dylan 2002

For someone like me who collects photos with celebrities, musician Bob Dylan is an absolute must. To be totally honest I hate Bob Dylan songs but there is no doubt that he is a legend. When Bob toured Australia in 2002 I first tried to meet him in Canberra, the capital of Australia, a three hour drive south of Sydney. On the day of his concert my girlfriend and I drove to Canberra and waited for Bob to leave the hotel. I chose Canberra because I knew there would be no other fans waiting for him there.

After a whole day of waiting I suddenly had a feeling that I should catch the lift down to the hotel's basement. As luck had it Bob's elevator opened at the very same time as ours and I calmly asked him for a photo. He ignored me. I then asked for an autograph, but still I was ignored. Three hours back up the highway and a few days later I was at Sydney Airport waiting for him to arrive. As the day went on more Dylan fans arrived at the airport until finally at 11pm when Bob arrived in Sydney there were about 30 fans waiting for him.

He got off the flight and his four security guards walked him straight through the main exit doors of the airport, then two of the guards blocked the fans from exiting through the doors. I was onto their plan though and I quickly walked through the doors with Bob. About seven other fans did as well. Bob took a pen off one of the fans and acted like he was going to sign items, but he didn't. He simply walked towards his waiting car. I tried my best to walk next to him while my girlfriend snapped a few photos.

As you can see it was a bit chaotic, but I did get myself in one of the photos. The guy next to me was his personal bodyguard. When Bob got into his car this security guard grabbed me and threatened to bash me. After a bit of pushing and shoving from both of us the guy eventually got in the car. It's not a posed photo, but it's still a photo with me and Bob Dylan—a lot of hard work though.

Brian Wilson 2002

For me and probably many other people, the Beach Boys band member Brian Wilson was almost a myth; someone we'd heard about but never actually got to see. This all changed for me in 2002 when Brian decided that he was going to tour again.

The first time I met him was by accident. I was at the airport one morning waiting for Pierce Brosnan to arrive when all of a sudden Brian Wilson walked off the flight. I got a very quick photo with him and then a few seconds later I saw Pierce.

When I had the photo developed it wasn't in focus so I tried for him a week later when he arrived back into Sydney. This time things weren't so rushed; he was very good to the fans and posed for photos and signed autographs, which changed from reading Brian Wilson to just signing BW a few minutes later.

Dennis Hopper 2002

I met actor Dennis Hopper in 2002 when he was in Sydney filming the movie *The Night We Called It a Day,* which was about Frank Sinatra's controversial tour of Sydney in the 1970s. I found out what hotel he was staying at and went down one day to try my luck. Well, luck was on my side as I had only waited about 15 minutes when I saw him walking around the foyer of the hotel.

I had a photo taken with him and had a chat to him about an Australian artist by the name of Norman Lindsay. I knew that Dennis was not only an art collector but an artist himself who used to hang out with Andy Warhol in the 1960s and 1970s. I suggested that he travel an hour or so north of Sydney to check out Norman's house and studio, which is now a museum. He told me that he had heard of Lindsay and he thanked me for the suggestion. I wonder if he ever ended up having a look at Lindsay's house?

Ian Richardson, Donald Sinden, Diana Rigg, Derek Jacobi 2002

It's always great to get a photo with one legend but snapping four in the same photo is almost unheard of. In 2002 these four British actors visited Sydney with their play *The Hollow Crown*. My friend Grayem Linton commissions artist Tony T to paint portraits of celebrities on car boots. My friend then meets the celebrities and gets these 'auto art' pieces signed.

On this particular day Grayem organised through the power of his boot lid for us to go backstage and meet all four actors so they could sign his art piece. They all very much liked the art piece and kindly signed it for him. We then had our photos taken with the car boot lid and the four actors. A very rare photo indeed.

Jay Kay 2002

When I was living in London in 2001 Jay Kay was everywhere. His music, his cars, his girlfriend and his funky hats were all talking points with my English friends. Jay Kay toured Australia in 2002 with his band Jamiroquai to sell-out shows.

The week he was in Sydney I received a bunch of phone calls from my female friends asking if they could meet him with me. After one of their concerts my girlfriend and I waited for him to return to his hotel. When he did he was great, he even took his trademark hat and glasses off for the photo.

Jerry Bruckheimer 2002

Producer Jerry Bruckheimer's name is everywhere; it seems that every time a television show's credits roll, his name appears. I sometimes wonder where he finds the time for his television and movie commitments.

I met him in 2002 when he was in Sydney with Ridley Scott to promote their movie *Black Hawk Down*. I had this photo taken with him as he arrived for the movie premiere. Jerry was very nice and obliging, while Ridley Scott was a bit more difficult to get a photo with, although I did eventually achieve success.

Jodie Foster 2002

I had read in the paper what day Jodie was arriving in Sydney to promote the movie *Panic Room*. My friend and I arrived at the international airport at about 5:30am for the LA flights that usually arrived between 6 and 7am. When the plane arrived I noticed that a few hired cars pulled up around a side area of the airport. A lot of celebrities use this side door to exit the airport to avoid the public.

My friend and I waited for Jodie to come through the side doors for about 45 minutes. We weren't too sure if she would give us a photo as she had just flown 13 hours from LA to Sydney. When she did come through the side doors she was very nice. She gave us a few photos and signed an item each for us. I would imagine that it would be a tough photo to get now because over the last few years she has taken herself out of the public eye and concentrated on being a mum. Good on her!

John Travolta 2002

John Travolta is a regular visitor to Sydney these days because he owns an original 1960s Qantas aeroplane. Qantas let him keep the original designs on the plane in exchange for John's promotional work for the Australian airline. On this trip in 2002 I went to his hotel and waited for him to leave. As I was waiting a few of his people came out the front of the hotel and asked me who I was waiting for. There was no point in lying to them so I told them: John Travolta. I then showed them two original 1970s records that John had released. They were so blown away with these records that they told me that John would love to see them, and when John came out of the hotel I was escorted over to him and showed him the records.

To be honest he'd probably seen them a few times over the years so it was no big deal for him but he was kind enough to sign them for me and give me this photo. After this photo John and his very large entourage went to a Sydney Swans football game. The ladies in the background of this photo are wearing Sydney Swans scarves.

Kirsten Dunst
and
Willam Dafoe 2002

In 2002 the photo agency I was working for called me and asked if I could cover the *Spider Man* press conference. I went to the press conference having no idea who was going to be there. When it started I was pleasantly surprised to see actors Kirsten Dunst, Willem Dafoe and Toby Maguire all sitting in front of me. Just as the press conference was about to start a bunch of the photographers who were protesting about not being able to cover certain events walked out, leaving only a handful of photographers to cover the event. I wasn't protesting about anything. In fact, I was very happy that I had a good chance of have my photo taken with three celebrities at once.

After the press conference I took a Spider Man toy glove from where the three stars were sitting and walked up on stage to see if I could have it signed. Kirsten and Willem were really nice and happily signed the toy hand and posed for this photo. Meanwhile the PR girls were panicking because I had approached the stars for an autograph. I yelled out to Toby and he hesitantly came over to me and signed the toy glove. When I asked him for a photo he said to me, 'You've got enough'. Needless to say I didn't get a photo with the notoriously fan-unfriendly Toby.

181 ★

Mel Gibson 2002

Without a doubt Mel Gibson is the hardest celebrity I have ever tried to get a photo with. I first met Mel accidentally in 1989 near his house in Sydney. I asked him then if I could have my photo taken with him, but he turned down my request. In my work as a photographer I have met Mel Gibson on numerous occasions, from 1990 onwards, but for some reason he would never pose for a photo with me.

In the mid 1990s I met Mel in Sydney at a restaurant. After dinner Mel left the restaurant and I asked him for a photo, and he said to me that there was no way in hell he was doing that for me. I then asked him if he would sign my original *Mad Max* movie poster. He got the pen scribbled on the poster and dropped the pen in the gutter for me to pick up. He completely ruined the poster.

My luck changed in 2002 when he was in Sydney to promote his movie *We Were Soldiers*. I was told by a photographer that Mel was having dinner at a restaurant. My friend and I waited for him to leave the restaurant and when he did we asked him for a photo. To my surprise he said, 'Sure'. I was so taken aback that my friend had to literally push me over to him so I could get the photo.

Roger Waters 2002

I met Pink Floyd's Roger Waters in 2002 when he was in Sydney to do some concerts. He was in a really good mood. I had brought a few posters to get signed but he wouldn't sign them for me. He told me that he didn't make any money from the sale of the posters so he wouldn't sign them. He didn't make any money from giving me a photo so I guess I'm lucky to have one. Lucky for me I brought a record with me which he happily signed.

The Dalai Lama 2002

The Dalai Lama had visited Sydney in the past but I never tried to meet him because I knew that there would be a lot of security around him. In 2002 I heard that he was doing a press conference at a Sydney hotel so I thought that I would try my luck at have my photo taken with him. I arrived just as the press conference was finishing and before I knew it the Dalai Lama came out of a room and was walking in my direction. I assessed the situation and noticed that he had three security guards at the front of him and three behind.

I used an old trick I had picked up in the late 1980s. As he and his security walked towards me I just stood my ground and didn't move. A few seconds later I found myself in the middle of his six security guards. I asked the Dalai Lama if I could have my photo taken with him and he put his right hand out and grabbed my hand. My friend, who had just left the press conference, snapped this photo for me. Within about four seconds it was all over. It was almost like a mini tornado had swept through the hotel foyer.

After he left the hotel a PR woman came running up to me and demanded to tell her who I was. I simply told her that I was Richard Simpkin. She then screamed, 'Who do you work for?' Once again I said Richard Simpkin. She then went on a rant and rave about how you cannot touch his Holiness. She was screaming this over and over again. I tried to tell her that he was the one that grabbed my hand in the first place but she would not listen. Eventually everyone in the hotel foyer, mostly media, started to laugh at her. She realised that she was making a fool out of herself and stormed off.

To be honest I didn't even realise that I had touched him. But photos don't lie; you can see my hand on his shoulder. I must have nervously done it as he was walking past me. But in my defence he held my hand first so I don't think I was entirely in the wrong by gently touching his shoulder. He had a huge smile on his face and I don't think it bothered him at all. You be the judge.

Will Smith 2002

Actor Will Smith was living in Sydney for a few months in 2002 because his wife Jada Pinkett Smith was filming *The Matrix* movies. I had met Will a few years before when he came to Sydney to promote the first *Men in Black* movie and found him to be really down to earth and very fan-friendly. I decided to try to meet him again after the premiere of the *Ali* movie.

I went to the after party and got a photo with Will giving me a hit to the head. Okay I'm only joking. He was simply doing what Ali used to do in photos— character acting at its best.

Andrew Johns
and
George Gregan 2003

To my knowledge this is the very first time that Andrew Johns, who was at the time the captain of the Australian Rugby League team, and George Gregan, who was captain of the Australian Rugby Union team, had ever met. And yours truly made it happen. I was waiting for Andrew at the hotel where he and the rest of the NSW State of Origin players were staying; by sheer coincidence the Australian Rugby Union team were also staying at the same hotel.

Andrew came down to the lobby and I noticed that George was also in the lobby talking with some team-mates. I asked Andrew if he had ever met George before and said he hadn't. I asked if he'd like to be introduced to him, and he said yes. So I walked over to where George was standing and I said, 'Excuse me, George, Andrew Johns would like to meet you.'

George must have thought that I was with Andrew and Andrew must have thought that I knew George. I have recently seen a photo of both of these sporting greats together at a function but I believe that this was their first meeting. You can tell by the look on their faces that they both felt a little awkward about meeting one another. I took full advantage of the moment and captured it with these two photos.

Bruce Springsteen 2003

I had met singer/songwriter Bruce a few years prior to this photo when he was in Sydney to do some small intimate shows. The photo that I had taken with him was terrible because the friend who took it cut off our heads! So when he came back to Sydney in 2003 I tried again.

My friend and I were waiting at the back of the hotel for him to arrive after his concert. Lucky for me I knew one of the band's drivers. He told me what time Bruce would be arriving at the hotel. When he did, two bodyguards got out of the van first and noticed that there was only two of us waiting for him. They told us that Bruce wasn't stopping for us, so not to bother asking for anything. Bruce got out of the van and came over to us and signed an art piece that my friend had and then he gave me this photo. Lucky for us he didn't listen to his bodyguards. Now you know why they call him 'The Boss'.

Buzz Aldrin 2003

Astronaut Buzz Aldrin was the second person to walk on the moon and I'm guessing he has a chip on his shoulder about not being the first. When he came to Sydney in 2003 I went to the airport and waited a few hours for him to arrive. I welcomed him to Australia and asked him if I could please have a photo with him. He started yelling at me that he doesn't do photos or autographs unless he gets paid. I was a little taken aback by his outburst, but I asked him how much he wanted to give me a photo. He then yelled at me again that I was being disrespectful to him. I didn't believe that I was, but in any case I left him alone.

The next day I went to a speech that he was doing in the city and asked him for a photo after he finished his speech—once again he was outraged. He told me that if I wanted a photo with him I would have to pay for it. I walked next to him as my friend snapped a photo of him yelling at me. A moment later I saw a large line of people waiting to meet Buzz, so I got in line. After a 20 minute wait a lady behind a cash register told me that it would cost $70 for a photo and autograph with Buzz. Part of the money was going to charity so I paid the money and got a photo with 'Mr Happy'.

I took my hat and glasses off so he wouldn't recognise me. It worked; he didn't recognise me and he has a slight grin in the photo. Was it worth the time, effort and the verbal abuse? Mmm. I sometimes wonder.

Christopher Reeve 2003

In 2003 Christopher Reeve was invited by the NSW State Government to come out to Sydney to promote stem cell research. He arrived in Sydney and was escorted by the police to his rented house. I had no intention of trying to meet him because of the security that he had. A few days into his stay I received a phone call from a friend of mine who was a first grade rugby league player for the Roosters football team, telling me that Christopher Reeve was going to visit the team that morning so his son could meet the players. My friend asked me if I wanted to meet Christopher. I jumped at the opportunity and met my friend at the training ground where he got me in.

Christopher and his son were meeting the players. I waited to the side for the players to have a photo taken with him, including former rugby league greats Ricky Stewart and Brad Fitler, and I then had my photo taken with him. He told me that he loved Sydney and he thought that it was a beautiful city. I found out a few days later that Christopher's son's nanny is Australian and they used to watch the Roosters play football on cable TV in the US.

Cold Chisel 2003

Cold Chisel is probably Australia's greatest band never to make it outside of Australia. Unlike INXS who conquered the world, Chisel's music very rarely left our shores. In 2003 Chisel were doing an Australian concert tour and I desperately wanted a group photo with them. I found out what time they were flying in from Perth and when front man Jimmy Barnes got off the flight I showed him a group photo of me with INXS and asked him if there would be any chance for me to get a Cold Chisel group photo.

   Jimmy simply said, 'Yeah sure', and as the other members of the band departed the plane Jimmy rounded them up for the photo. But just as I was about to have the photo taken, the band's drummer Steve Prestwich yelled out, 'Hang on! I've left my wallet on the plane.' He ran back down onto the plane and went searching for his wallet. A few minutes passed and the band members started to get a bit restless and wanted to retrieve their luggage. I had a few records to have signed so I quickly pulled them out and asked each member to sign away. Eventually Steve found his wallet and returned to the group and I was able to get this very rare photo. If you're a Chisel fan then you'll really appreciate this photo.

Darryl Hannah 2003

Actor Darryl came to Sydney in 2003 to promote the movie *Kill Bill Volume I*. The star of the movie, Uma Thurman, was supposed to do the promo visit but cancelled the day before. I went to the airport and met Darryl as she got off the flight from the US. I really like this photo because she is holding a teddy bear. Darryl told me that her bear kept her company during the 13-hour flight. I wonder what they spoke about?

David and Victoria Beckham 2003

In 2003 my girlfriend and I were holidaying in LA and on our last day we went to a hotel in Beverly Hills to simply wait in the lobby to see if we could 'bump into' any wandering celebrities. After 30 minutes or so the doors of the hotel opened and ten or so bodyguards walked into the hotel. At first I couldn't see who they were protecting, but as they walked in our direction I spotted 'Posh 'n' Becks'.

Victoria walked into the hotel's restaurant first, leaving David with no security. I asked David for a photo and he happily obliged. Twenty minutes later Victoria walked outside to the lobby to use the toilet. I asked her if I could have a photo with them both when they were leaving. She said yes and about an hour later they both left the restaurant. Their security moved out of the way so David and Victoria could walk straight over to us. They could not have been any nicer.

Debbie Harry 2003

I first met Blondie's Debbie Harry in Sydney in 1990 at a press conference. After the press conference was over Debbie signed a few photos for me and even added a lipstick kiss to one of them. I treasure that photo. Thirteen years later Debbie was back in Sydney with her band and I met her again at the airport. Debbie was very good to the fans that were waiting for her and even gave a few of them kisses. She spent about ten minutes signing autographs and posing for photos. After being an international rock goddess for 30 years or more, Debbie is still great to all her loyal and loving fans.

Duran Duran 2003

During the 1980s Duran Duran was one of the biggest bands in the world. In 1990 they visited Sydney on a promotional trip and I was lucky enough to get a group photo with them, but when I had my film processed I was disappointed to find that I had set the film exposure incorrectly and none of the photos turned out.

In 2003 Duran Duran were back in Sydney and this time I had my camera set correctly. A friend of mine is a huge fan of the band and followed them around Australia, and he was trying to organise a group photo with them. Eventually he got all five members of the band together when they were leaving Sydney Airport. He got his group photo and lucky for me so did I.

Geoffrey Rush 2003

In my opinion Geoffrey Rush is one of the best actors in the world today. His performances in *Shine, Quills, Frida and The Life and Death of Peter Sellers* I believe justify my claim. Although Geoffrey is an Academy Award winning actor he somehow doesn't fit into the 'celebrity' category; he sits more comfortably in the 'actor' category.

I have met Geoffrey twice in Sydney and on both occasions he has been the perfect gentleman. When I took this photo of him in 2003 I asked him to sign a poster for the movie *Frida*. He kindly did so, and to my surprise had not seen the poster before. I always presumed that these actors would have seen most of their movie paraphernalia especially something like a movie poster, but I guess some of them lead such busy lives they don't have a chance to.

Harrison Ford 2003

In 2003 my girlfriend and I went to the US for our 10th anniversary. I had promised her that we wouldn't try to meet any celebrities on this trip but when I heard that Harrison was going to unveil his star on the Hollywood walk of fame I couldn't resist trying to meet him. As fate had it we caught the wrong bus and missed the whole ceremony. I then called a fellow autograph collector and found out which restaurant Harrison was at.

I arrived the restaurant to find about 30 fans waiting for Harrison. When he came out all of the fans just stood there as they didn't want to get him angry and ruin any chance of an autograph. After about 30 seconds I broke away from the group and walked up to him. I asked him for a photo, but he said he would only sign one autograph per fan. I had nothing to have signed but once he said those words all of the fans rushed over to him. He signed one autograph per person and I just stood there and watched. When he had finished I told him that I didn't have anything autographed and all I wanted was a photo. He thought about it for a second and let me have the photo taken with him.

The fans couldn't believe it as he very rarely gives photos to fans. The next day when I had the film developed I was in total shock to find out the film was somehow faulty and none of the photos turned out. Then for some reason my luck changed. It was the last day in LA and a friend of mine was going to drop us at the airport. We were a few hours ahead of schedule so he suggested that we sit at a hotel in Beverly Hills to see if we could see any wandering celebs. In two hours I had my photo taken with Kate Hudson, Macy Gray, Elvis Costello, Larry Flynt, David and Victoria Beckham and Harrison Ford. If that photo turned out the first time I wouldn't have collected the other celeb shots. Not bad for a lazy two hours in LA.

Ian Thorpe 2003

I took this photo of Ian at the airport. The media were interviewing him before he and the rest of the Australian swimming team were about to leave for a swimming meet in Germany. While he was answering questions from the media, I stood in the middle of the journalists and took some photos with my instamatic. I was very surprised when I had my film developed and saw that I had this photo of Ian. It was sheer luck that he is smiling and looking straight down my lens.

Jack Black 2003

Funny guy Jack Black was in Sydney in 2003 to promote his movie *School of Rock*. He was doing an interview at Fox Studios so I went to the studios to see if I could have a photo taken with him after his interview. The security guard that was with him started to freak out when I approached his prized star. Jack told the guy to, 'Relax, man.' I got the photo and he then walked around the corner to the premiere of the movie. I walked up to have a look at the premiere and was a little surprised to see only a handful of fans waiting for him to arrive. To his credit he stopped for the fans and gave them all autographs and photos.

Jeff Bridges 2003

Only in LA. I was there with my girlfriend on a holiday and we were in Hollywood Boulevard doing the tourist thing. As we were crossing the road I noticed actor Jeff Bridges walking towards me pushing an old lady in a wheelchair. Without even thinking about it I asked him for a photo in the middle of the road; pure instinct. He was kind enough to pause for a moment so I could have a photo taken with him. I didn't even have time to take off my sun glasses. It was all over in two seconds and both parties continued on their separate ways.

Kate Hudson 2003

I was in LA in 2003 and had two hours to kill before I had to be at the airport, so my friend suggested that I wait at a hotel in Beverly Hills to see who I could find. As soon as I walked into the hotel lobby I noticed actor Kate Hudson standing there talking to some people. When she finished talking I asked her for a photo, but she told me that she didn't have time. About an hour later she walked past me and again I asked her for a photo, adding that it would only take a few seconds. She agreed and I got the shot.

Celebrities sometimes have excuses for not wanting to give fans photos or autographs. I've heard them all before: 'I'm in a rush', 'I'll do it later for you', in the hope that you won't ask them later. My all-time favourite is when they're at the international airport just about to leave the country and they say to you, 'I'll do it next time.' They then get on the plane and nine out of ten times you never see them again.

Keanu Reeves 2003

I had met Keanu in 1995 so I didn't need to meet him again, but a friend of mine is a huge fan of his and she wanted to meet him. I went down to the hotel he was staying at for *The Matrix* movie premiere. At the hotel I noticed a large boat with security all around it, so it wasn't too difficult to work out that this was the boat that *The Matrix* stars were going to travel on to get to the premiere at the Sydney Opera House.

Keanu's co-star, Hugo Weaving, came out first and gave us a photo. A minute later Jada Pinkett Smith left for the boat. She wouldn't do any photos for us and even went to the degree of telling her bodyguards to stop us from approaching her. Keanu came out and he was great. He made my friend's day by giving her a photo and an autograph. I updated my photo with him as well. I like the Sydney Opera House in the background.

Keith Richards 2003

The members of the Rolling Stones are extremely hard to meet, so when my friend, Grayem Linton, told me that he was trying to organise a backstage meeting with them I was relieved. Grayem commissions celebrities' portraits to be painted onto car boot lids, what he calls 'auto art', then asks celebs to autograph their portraits.

In 2003 the Stones toured Sydney and my friend had a boot lid commissioned of Keith Richards. He got in contact with the promoter Paul Dainty and organised a meeting for him to go backstage to meet Keith. I went along with him so I could take the photos. Once backstage Paul asked us to follow him, and we walked along a long corridor and approached these huge black curtains. Paul walked through the curtains and as we tried to walk through a security guard stopped us. Paul turned around and told the guy that we were guests of the band. I almost felt like royalty. Paul then walked us through the curtains, told us we had ten minutes, then left.

There before our eyes was Keith, sitting on a stool with a cigarette hanging out of the side of his mouth as he played his white electric guitar. Grayem and I didn't say a word, instead we just watched. After a minute or so Keith looked up and apologised for not seeing us straight away. He told us to sit with him on a lounge so he could see the artwork. He loved it and called Ronnie Wood over to take a look. We got to spend about ten minutes with Keith and Ronnie. After our meeting with the rock and roll legends Paul Dainty gave us two tickets to the show. What a night! I wasn't even a Rolling Stones fan, but I am now.

LeAnn Rimes and Keith Urban 2003

Singers LeAnn and Keith toured Sydney together in 2003. Keith, who is one of Australia's favourite home-grown stars, is one of the nicest celebs I have ever met. I'm a huge INXS fan and so one day when I was looking at the credits to an INXS song called 'Shining Star' I noticed Keith Urban's name credited as a backing singer. I wondered if it was the same Keith Urban. So after their concert I met them both at their hotel and had this photo taken. I then asked Keith if he'd sung backing vocals on the INXS song and he said he had. I told him that I had the single in my car and asked if he'd sign it in the next day or two. He told me that they were both going across the road to the pub for a drink with the band and my friend and I were welcome to join them. I retrieved the single from my car and Keith signed it for me. We then stuck around and had a chat with him.

Lou Reed 2003

Musician Lou Reed toured Australia in 2003 and I went along with a friend to the airport to try and meet him. My friend, who is a huge fan, actually met Lou in the early 1970s when Lou was in Sydney and he even had a photo with him to prove it.

Lou got off the flight and my friend asked Lou if he would sign his 30-year-old photo. Lou took the pen and just did circles on the photo. My friend then went on to tell Lou exactly what he had said 30 years ago when he was at a Sydney press conference. Lou started to realise that my friend was a huge fan so he asked for the photo back and dedicated the photo to him. Mind you he didn't fix the horrible autograph. After a chat we asked him for a photo.

I commented that my friend needed an update as it had been 30 years. Lou agreed to the photo but added that I couldn't use flash. Just as I was about to take the photo with him and my friend, Lou jumped out of the photo and said, 'No flash!' I informed him that I had the flash turned off. I took the photo and then got one for myself. Lou must have felt bad that he was a bit rude to my friend because he gave him a free ticket to his show that night.

Marcel Marceau 2003

There are only a few celebrities in the world who are truly one of a kind. Mime artist Marcel Marceau is one of them; he's the only person who comes to mind when you think of a mime artist, isn't he? So when he toured Sydney in 2003 I definitely wanted to have a photo taken with him, preferably with his make-up on.

I met Marcel at the airport and tried to organise a photo with him in make-up. His PR lady said maybe after the show. I then went to a book signing and asked the PR lady again, she said she would try her best. I went to the show and after the performance the PR lady had all of the fans who were waiting for his autograph give her their items for him to sign backstage. She then told me that there was no time for my photo with him in make-up.

When he left the venue the PR lady told the waiting fans that Marcel wasn't stopping for photos as he was very tired. Lucky for me she told Marcel to pose with me for this photo. He did have a bit of face make-up left on. She apologised and told me that it was the best that she could do. I wasn't complaining I was thrilled at the chance to meet the great man.

Martina Navratilova 2003

I first met tennis champ Martina in January 1989 when she was in Sydney to play a tennis tournament. I waited for her with about ten other kids to finish her game and when she did we all asked her for an autograph. One of the kids gave her a pen that didn't work so when she tried to give us autographs she couldn't. She then gave the pen back to the kid and said, 'Next time give me a pen that works,' and with that she was off. I learnt a lesson that day: always have a back-up pen with me!

In 2003 Martina was in Sydney yet again, this time for a charity event. When she arrived she wouldn't give me a photo. Martina came out of the event to use the toilets so I asked her for the photo. She told me that she would only give me one after the event. Five hours later the event was over and I finally got this shot with her.

Naomi Watts and Heath Ledger 2003

In 2003 my girlfriend and I were in LA on yet another holiday (don't worry we do go to other places). We were with a few Aussie friends and we decided to go to the movies. When we got to the movies I noticed actor couple Naomi and Heath standing in the line to buy a ticket. I thought, being a fellow Aussie, I would go up and say hi.

After a conversation about Sydney and Heath's movie about Aussie bushranger Ned Kelly I asked them if I could have a photo taken with them. Heath was a bit hesitant but Naomi couldn't care less. I then said to Heath, 'Did I mention that I thought you were really good in Ned Kelly?' He gave me a half grin and agreed to the photo.

Paris and Nikki Hilton 2003

I first saw Paris and Nikki on television in 2002 in a story about them being the new 'IT' girls. The story covered a day in the life of the Hilton girls, which included shopping, socialising, shopping again and then clubbing. As the year progressed I kept seeing stories on the Hilton sisters.

So in 2003 when they both came out to Sydney I thought that I would get a photo with them just for fun. I met them as they arrived for *The Matrix* premiere at the Sydney Opera House. I told them that before I had the photo taken I would have to put my sunglasses on because they were party girls. They gave me a small giggle and then the photo. A few days after I met them, Paris was in the headlines because of a certain video that had surfaced. After that Paris became a superstar and Nikki became…well, Paris's sister.

Pete Townshend 2003

The Who musos Pete Townshend and Roger Daltry toured Sydney together in 2003. I had met Roger a few years before so I didn't need to try for him again. I focused on Pete. I waited for him to come back to his hotel after a concert and had this photo taken with him. I was only one of three people to get a photo with him because I found out from some friends in Melbourne that after their Melbourne gig they drove directly to the airport and flew back to Sydney. They didn't stop for anyone in Melbourne. After Sydney they left the country so I guess I was lucky I got Pete at all.

Quentin Tarantino 2003

I met writer/director Quentin at the Sydney international airport in 2003 when he flew out here to promote the movie *Kill Bill Volume I*. He arrived on the same flight as Darryl Hannah and when I met him he was very nice and down to earth. The security guard told me not to approach him at the airport, but that I should try to meet him at the movie premiere. This was a bad suggestion as at movie premieres there are sometimes hundreds of screaming fans. Because there was only my friend and I at the airport we tried a little harder.

Quentin agreed with me that it would be much easier for not only me but him as well to give me a photo and an autograph. It took about ten seconds and it was all over. One on one is always the way to go, if you know how to do it.

Ray Charles 2003

I had met musician Ray Charles a few times over the years and always found him rude. Now, I knew he was blind so I never asked him for an autograph, but I used to ask him for a photo. I always got the same response, which was Ray ignoring me. I would rather someone tell me no than be ignored.

In 2003 I met him again after his concert at his hotel. I approached him and said to him that his performance was one of the best I had ever seen. He stood at the lift with his carer and just faced the lift door until it opened and he was escorted in. All I wanted from him was a response. As usual I didn't get one so I thought I'd put Ray Charles into the 'too hard' category.

About a week later I was at the airport waiting for Bob Dylan to arrive when I noticed Ray get off a flight. He was just standing there as his entourage were working out what they were doing. I said to my girlfriend, 'Come over with me and when I stand next to Ray just take the photo.' I walked up to Ray, stood next to him and my girlfriend snapped the photo. I didn't say a word to him. I know it was a bit cheeky of me but it was the only way.

Rob Lowe 2003

In 1990 while I was hanging out with INXS at their recording studios actor Rob Lowe visited the guys. I was lucky enough to have a photo taken with Rob, Jon Farriss (INXS drummer) and Michael Hutchence. In 2003 I heard that Rob was coming to Australia to shoot a movie and he was also going to be a special guest at the horse races for a particular gala day. I went to the races and after clearing four security checks I got into the VIP area where Rob was. The PR girls told me not to approach Rob as he didn't want to be bothered by the media, but I could photograph the other celebrities. After about ten minutes of walking around this VIP area and seeing 'celebs' like radio DJs, hairdressers and a few wannabe socialites, I noticed Rob siting at the front of the tent waiting for the next race to start.

I took the photo of Rob, Michael Hutchence, Jon Farriss and me out of my bag and walked up to Rob. His security told me to go away, but I was able to show Rob the photo. He got up off his chair and couldn't believe that I had this photo. He told me that after it was taken the three of them went to Kings Cross and he got a tattoo while he was extremely drunk. He told me that he missed his friend Michael Hutchence very much and he simply couldn't get over that it was me in the photo with them.

He asked me to go over to his wife at the bar and show her, but added, 'Come back to me after you show my wife.' I showed his wife and walked back over to Rob, who asked me to have a drink with him, so his bodyguard went and got us drinks. You should have seen the look on the PR girls' faces when they saw me hanging out with Rob Lowe. After about 30 minutes I thanked Rob for his time, had a photo taken with him and left the so-called VIP area.

Rose Byrne 2003

If Rose Byrne doesn't make it in Hollywood then I
don't know what's wrong. She's a great actor with
beauty, personality and screen presence: Hollywood
wake up! Okay, so I'm a big Rose Byrne fan. I first saw
her in the 1999 movie *Two Hands*. Since then she's
appeared in movies such as *Troy, Star Wars: Episode
II* and *Marie Antoinette* (gee, I think I should be her
PR). As I was taking her photo, I noticed that Rose was
uncomfortable posing, so I said 'Come on, Rose, make
the photo fun'. She pulled this funny expression and
made the photo fun. Now that's a great actor. Okay I'll
stop now.

Rudolph Giuliani 2003

Former New York mayor Giuliani came to Sydney in 2003 to promote his autobiography. I met him at the airport when he arrived and was pushed away by his security team. There was definitely no chance of a photo that morning. The next day he was doing a book signing in the city. My friend and I bought his book and waited in line with everyone else. When it came time to meet him my friend asked him if she could have a photo taken with him and he happily agreed. After my friend's photo his American security guard told me not to ask him for a photo. So I immediately asked him for the photo. Giuliani had no problem with it so I posed next to him on stage.

When I left the bookstore his security guard followed me outside and demanded I hand over the film. I informed him that Giuliani was doing a public book signing and he agreed to have his photo taken with the public. This guy wouldn't let it go and he tried to grab the camera out of my hand. I informed him that he was in my country on a tourist visa and if he tried to touch me again I would call the police. I told him to let it go and I quickly got out of there before another one of his minders got heavy-handed with me. You see, it wasn't about the photo, it was about this guy losing control of the situation.

Sir Edmund Hillary 2003

In 2003 it was 50 years since Edmund and Tenzing Norgay first climbed Mt Everest. Edmund was the guest of honour at a dinner to mark the occasion. The room was packed with a couple of hundred people and I can tell you that during the night Edmund signed autographs for every single person. I had this photo taken with him just after he made his speech.

Tony Bennett 2003

Entertainer Tony Bennett had been out to Sydney on a number of occasions but for some reason I had never bothered to meet him. In 2003 he came back to Sydney with k.d. lang. I had tried for k.d. a few years prior to this attempt and as always she wouldn't stop for a photo with anyone. Actually I asked her for an autograph once and she signed my items 'Madonna', 'Mariah Carey' and 'Celine Dion'. She gave them back and said, 'There you go, you got a few different ones.'

The day that she arrived with Tony, a mother with her child noticed k.d. and asked if she would pose with her young daughter, but k.d. refused the request. On the other side of the coin Tony was absolutely great. He posed with anyone who asked and signed autographs for fans. Maybe k.d. should take a leaf out of Tony's book. After all, he's stood the test of time.

Al Pacino 2004

I met actor Al Pacino when I was in Los Angeles filming a documentary about how I meet celebrities. My girlfriend, who was also the cameraperson, and my friend were waiting at Mr Chow's restaurant, where many of the world's celebs go to dine. On this particular night Al Pacino had turned up to have dinner. Lucky we were there when Pacino arrived, as he posed for photos with me, my friend and two other people that were waiting. Within a short amount of time the word had spread like wildfire that Pacino was at the restaurant.

By the time Pacino went inside the restaurant, there were about 50 fans waiting for him. It was pure mayhem, but to his credit he handled the situation like a true professional. He got into his car and signed autographs for over ten minutes. When he left, a few fans followed him in their cars, and when they returned told the few of us who were still at the restaurant that when Pacino stopped at the traffic lights the fans jumped out of their cars and asked him for photos and autographs. Pacino got out of his car and posed for photos. What a star!

Anastacia 2004

Songstress Anastacia had been to Sydney on a number of occasions but I had never had the chance to meet her and all my friends had always told me how nice she was. When I was in LA in 2004 and saw her leaving a nightclub I asked her for a photo. She kindly said yes but the bouncer from the club told her not to pose with me. My friend took the photo of her trying to pose with me while the club's bouncer is pulling her to the car.

You can see how awkward she is feeling with this guy pulling her. I kind of felt sorry for her as he made both of us feel so uncomfortable. In my opinion if the celebrity wants to do a photo or an autograph for a fan then it should be up to them and not other people.

Angela Lansbury 2004

When I went over to LA in 2004 I really wanted to meet three actors: Michael Douglas, Peter Falk and Angela Lansbury. I was lucky to have met all three but unfortunately I couldn't get a photo with Michael Douglas. I was at an Academy Awards luncheon that was doubling as a tribute luncheon for Ann Miller (who had recently passed away) at the Beverly Hilton Hotel. There were a lot of Hollywood legends at the luncheon to honour Miller, including Angela Lansbury. When Angela left the luncheon she told the fans that were waiting for her that she wasn't stopping for any of them. I had flown halfway around the world and I was not going to miss this opportunity.

I followed Angela through the car park of the hotel and explained to her that I probably would never get the chance to meet her again and could I please have a photo with her. She said, 'You're not being very nice to me.' I knew that I wasn't being rude to her. In fact I was treating her with the utmost respect. She eventually took a deep breath and told me I could have a photo with her. When I went back downstairs and told my friends that she had let take me a photo, they were all a bit shocked as she was renowned as a tough one to get.

Avril Lavigne 2004

When singer Avril had come to Sydney on two previous occasions, a friend of mine tried for an autograph and a photo with her but she wouldn't do either. So when I was in LA in 2004 and saw a few flashes going off outside a nightclub I pulled my car over and went to have a look. To my surprise it was Avril signing autographs and posing for photos.

Just as she was about to go into the club I quickly got this photo with her. I have no idea who the other guy in the photo is, but he sure looks happy! The strange thing was that when Avril came back out to Sydney a few months later she refused to sign my photo.

Bianca Jagger 2004

I am a huge Andy Warhol fan, so when I saw model
Bianca Jagger standing outside a restaurant in Beverly
Hills I asked her for a photo with the idea of asking her
about her time partying with Warhol in the 1970s.

I put my arm around her because I think it makes for
a better photo, but when I did she said to me, 'Don't
touch me!' I apologised for doing so and awkwardly
stood next to her for the photo. Needless to say I didn't
ask her about Warhol.

Bob Denver 2004

When I was in LA I heard that on one particular night there was going to be a DVD launch party for the *Gilligan's Island* television show. I was told that Bob Denver who played Gilligan in the classic show, was going to be at the DVD launch.

When I got to the venue, which was about an hour's drive from Beverly Hills I soon found out that there was no area to wait to meet the stars unless you were media. I went up to the PR desk and told the ladies that I was from Australia and I wanted a place on the red carpet to interview the stars. 'Who do you work for?' they asked me. 'Richard Simpkin TV,' I replied. Now they didn't have a clue who I was. All they knew was that I was a guy with a video camera from Australia. And you know what—it actually worked!

I got my very own place on the red carpet with a sticker in front of me that said 'Richard Simpkin TV Australia'. As the stars from the show walked down the red carpet they were introduced to me, I asked them a few questions then finished the interview by telling them that I always have a photo taken with my guests.

When I interviewed Bob I noticed that he was wearing Ugh boots. The first question asked him was, 'Bob, I see you're wearing Ugh boots.' He said to me, 'Yeah, I am. How did you notice that?' I told him I was from Australia and Ugh boots are very Australian. He then told me that the Ugh boots that he was wearing were from Australia and that he gets them imported. The PR girls had no idea what I was talking to him about, but I can tell you I got the best interview out of him that night. And of course I ended the interview with a photo. Now that's a wrap.

Carrie Fisher

The first thing I was about to say to Carrie when I saw her was, 'Oh my God, what happened to Princess Leia and what have you done with her?' I went to a book signing of hers and waited for the very small crowd to leave the store. After she finished signing her book I asked her to sign a *Star Wars* item for me, but the staff in the store told me that she was only signing her book.

So I waited outside for her to leave. About five minutes later she left the store with a friend and came over to me to sign my Star Wars item. I then had a photo taken with her. She was very kind.

Cate Blanchett 2004

I met actor Cate Blanchett at the very first 'G'day LA' Australia Week Festival in 2004. I had met Cate back in Sydney in 1999, but when I saw her in LA she was pregnant and looked just beautiful. I got a quick photo with her before she was rushed into the dinner. It was a great night to get a lot of famous Aussies, because it was the very first 'G'day LA' day dinner to be held and there were no other fans waiting for celebs like Cate Blanchett, Olivia Newton-John or Anthony LaPaglia.

Charlize Theron 2004

While I was in LA in February 2004 I went to the Beverly Hilton Hotel to have a look at which celebs were attending a luncheon for the Academy Awards. When I arrived it had already started so I waited. When it finished I met a number of celebs as they were leaving, from Julie Andrews to Alec Baldwin. I went down to the pool area where Ben Kingsley, Elvis Costello, Sofia Coppola and actor Charlize Theron were all doing interviews. I soon realised that the hotel security guards were throwing out any autograph collectors who were hovering around the pool.

I said to my girlfriend and friend that we needed to pretend to act like hotel guests. We sat by the pool and acted like we were sunbaking while pretending to sip drinks that were already there from the guests before us. The plan worked. Every time the security did a scope of the area we raised the level of our voices so they knew we were foreigners. After Charlize finished her interviews we got up from our poolside chairs and had a photo taken with her. We were also lucky enough to get the other celebs after they had finished their interviews.

Cyd Charisse and Tony Martin 2004

I met Hollywood legend Cyd Charisse, who starred alongside such greats as Gene Kelly in *Singin' in the Rain* (1952) and Fred Astaire in *The Band Wagon* (1953) in the mid 1990s when she came to Sydney as a special guest for an event.

The day I met her she gave me an autograph but wouldn't stop for a photo telling me that it was too windy. In 2004 I met the Hollywood legend again but this time it was inside a hotel and lucky for me there was no wind. Cyd was with her husband Tony Martin, who is also a Hollywood legend, so it was great to get two legends in the one photo.

Debbie Reynolds 2004

In January/February 2004 I was in LA filming a documentary about how I meet celebrities. Debbie Reynolds was performing *Love Letters* at the San Fernando Valley Playhouse. I waited for her to arrive at the stage door, and when she did she invited me, my girlfriend and my friend into the theatre and gave us a tour of the backstage area. The following night we were invited to a private cocktail party, where we met Debbie again and her co-star John Saxon.

Diane Keaton 2004

In certain hotels in LA if you wait around the lobby for a while there is a good chance of seeing a celebrity or two. I was in LA in 2004 and I went to a hotel to see who I could find. In a short time I noticed actor Diane Keaton walking towards the lifts, and I walked over and asked her for a photo. She was fine with the photo but as I was posing with her I felt her hand push against my chest. She was trying to push me out of the photo.

My friend asked her for a photo, but just as I was about to take the shot she quickly turned away from the camera. I told her that she moved so we needed to do another photo. 'Oh I'm sorry,' replied Diane. We did another photo and the same thing happened again. When we had the photos developed we noticed that in both of my friends' photos she had turned her face as I took them and you couldn't make out who it was. If you have a look at this photo you can see her pushing me in the side of my chest. Very strange indeed.

Dick Van Dyke 2004

Ah! Dick Van Dyke, what a star. I grew up watching *Chitty Chitty Bang Bang* and to this day it is one of my all-time favourite movies. I met Dick a few days before this photo was taken in downtown LA. He was launching a new development block for the homeless. I was a little nervous about meeting him as I didn't want to be disappointed—just in case he wasn't nice. But my concerns were quickly forgotten when I met him. He is simply one of the nicest people I have ever met.

Like everyone else that day I rambled on about how much I enjoyed watching him at the movies or on television. He was so kind and gracious with his time and spoke to me for about 20 minutes. At the end of the day I asked him if he could sing the song 'Chitty Chitty Bang Bang' for me on video. Without any hesitation Dick sang the song for me while a crowd gathered around to watch and listen. When he finished everyone gave him a huge round of applause. I was fortunate to meet him again at a luncheon in Hollywood a few days later where I had this photo taken with him. A fan gave him a *Chitty Chitty Bang Bang* comic; he is holding it up in the photo.

Dustin Hoffman 2004

When I was in LA in January and February of 2004 I went down to a LA Lakers basketball game. When the game finished I waited with about 20 other autograph collectors at the side of the stadium to see which celebrities were at the game. We were all waiting at the valet area because celebrity or not, everyone who had their car in valet had to wait for it.

I noticed Dustin leaving the game and asked him for a photo, and he said to me that he would do it at his car. I walked over to his car with him and when we got to the car he discovered that his son had forgotten to get the keys from the valet. He started to bang his hands on top of his car and rock backwards and forwards. I'm not joking here; I can honestly tell you that he was acting like Rain Man.

His son took a few minutes to get the keys and he started to act very weird. I stood next to him and just waited for him to get into the car as he was obviously starting to panic with all of the attention—there were now about 20 people surrounding his car for an autograph. When he got in his car he calmed down and started to sign autographs for the waiting crowd. After the autographs I had a photo taken with him as he was just about to drive off. It was very strange to see him act in this way.

Sarah Ferguson 2004

I went to the airport the day after the Golden Globes in 2004 to see if I could meet any celebs as they were leaving LA. After a few hours of waiting the only celebrity that I saw was Fergie. I walked up to her and asked her for a photo, but just as I was about to have a photo taken with her this very big security guard told me to take my Hustler baseball cap off as it would not look right in a photo with the former royal. I quickly removed my cap and got this photo with her.

Harry Belafonte 2004

The first night that I arrived in LA in January 2004 I went to Mr Chow's restaurant to see if I could meet any celebs. After an unfruitful hour I asked a waiting photographer if she knew if any celebs were inside the restaurant. She told me that she didn't know but added that I should go to the Beverly Hilton Hotel as the crooner Harry Belafonte was accepting an award to honour his life.

I hit the ground running and when I arrived at the hotel I told my friend to follow me and walked straight into the ballroom to find Harry Belafonte on the stage with the entire room giving him a standing ovation. I walked through the room full of people dressed in their very best evening clothes and walked straight up on stage.

The room was still applauding him. As the applause trailed off I walked up to him and said, 'Mr Belafonte, my name is Richard Simpkin and I have come from Australia to celebrate this wonderful night with you.' He was a little taken aback. I shook his hand and had a photo taken with him on stage in front of a packed ballroom. I'm sure he must have been thinking, 'My God, this guy came all the way from Australia and he didn't even to bother to bring his suit.' .

Sir Ian McKellen 2004

I said to myself in early 2004 that when I returned from spending four weeks in LA I wasn't going to go after anymore celebs for that year. So when actor Sir Ian was in Sydney in early January 2004 I decided that I would meet him just before I left for LA; you might say it was a warm-up for the trip. I met Ian after he finished one of his performances in the play *Dance of Death*.

I was waiting with a few other fans that were *The Lord of the Rings* enthusiasts. Ian had attracted a whole new audience after he appeared in those movies. He was extremely good to all who were waiting for him, giving everyone autographs and photos.

Jamie Foxx 2004

I met Jamie in early 2004 while he was waiting for his car at a Grammy's function in LA. Now, this was before he had won an Academy Award for the Ray Charles movie so he wasn't a huge star. As I was speaking with him his manager said to me, 'Are you from Australia?' 'Yes,' I replied. He then went on to tell me that he and Jamie were just about to go to Sydney where Jamie was going to star in the movie *Stealth*. He asked me if I had a boat. I told him that I did and he then asked me for my phone number because he wanted me to take him and Jamie out on the harbour in Sydney.

I gave him my number and a few weeks later Jamie was in Sydney. I didn't receive a phone call from them, but I guessed they got their own boat. I did see Jamie in Sydney a few weeks later and he had no recollection of our conversation in LA. And I thought that we were going to be friends, damn.

John Cleese 2004

When I was living in London in 2001 I was told by a few autograph collectors that John was going to leave England because he was sick of all of the attention that he received in his home country and he was also sick of fans knocking on his door for autographs. Now I don't know how true these stories are but I do know that when I met him outside Mr Chow's restaurant in Beverly Hills in 2004 he was as happy as could be about signing autographs.

The night that I met him I was waiting at the restaurant with about 20 Americans, two Germans and my girlfriend and friend. When John left the restaurant only we Aussies and the Germans initially went up to him. I had been a huge fan of *Fawlty Towers* as a kid so I was thrilled to meet him. The American autograph collectors decided that they also better get his autograph. He told everyone to stand in a line and he would sign autographs for everyone. Because he was calm, everyone else was calm and it made the whole process very easy and relaxed.

Julie Andrews 2004

I had arrived at a Hollywood luncheon at the Beverly Hilton Hotel just as it had started. When I arrived I asked a few autograph collectors who had gone in. They told me a few celebs had stopped but added that Julie Andrews wouldn't stop on the way in; however, she did say that she would do autographs on the way out. When she left the luncheon she walked straight passed the fans and told them that she wasn't signing for anyone. I knew that this would be my one and only chance to ever meet the star of *Mary Poppins* and *The Sound of Music*, and I wanted to try and have a photo taken with her.

I left the foyer of the hotel and went outside. I very quickly explained to Julie that I didn't want her autograph but wanted a photo with her. I was from Australia and this would be my only chance to ever meet her. She just gave me a smirk and looked at my friend as if to say to him, take the photo. My friend did and I added another Hollywood legend to my collection.

Juliette Lewis 2004

It was the night of the Golden Globes and I was outside the official party in LA with about 100 autograph collectors, 15 photographers and a beefed-up security team. All the big names were at the party, from Nicole Kidman to Michael Douglas. The party was at a restaurant, surrounded by barricades to keep the fans at bay. Most of the celebs were getting out of their cars and walking straight through the security area. But not Juliette. She walked through the fan area to get inside the party.

A handful of people had photos with her. As she was making her way closer to the entrance the security noticed her and a few of them surrounded her to get her inside. I yelled out, 'Juliette, I'm from Australia. Can I get a photo with you?' She turned around and said to the security, 'I'm gonna do a photo with this guy because he's from Australia'. Thank God for Australia; the Aussie accent does wonders for me in LA.

Karl Malden 2004

There aren't too many Hollywood legends left so when I meet one it is always a huge honour. I was at a luncheon in Beverly Hills in 2004 to see which celebs were leaving the luncheon. I asked an autograph collector if he could spot anyone worth going for, and he told me that he couldn't but added that actor Karl Malden was waiting outside for his car. He then added, 'You don't want him, he's too old.'

I quickly left the luncheon and ran outside where Karl was waiting with his wife for their car to be dropped off by the valet. In 1951 Karl won an Academy Award for best supporting actor in the classic *A Streetcar Named Desire*, but it was his television appearances that most people remember him for. He was the star of the hit show *The Streets of San Francisco*, and I remember him in the American Express ads, which he did for 21 years.

I walked up to him and asked for a photo. He was very kind and gracious and gave me a photo adding that he loved Australia and he would love to get back down there for a holiday. I was in mid conversation with him when my girlfriend yelled out to me that Angela Lansbury (*Murder She Wrote*) was leaving the luncheon. I had to quickly finish the conversation with him and try to catch Angela. Only in LA!

Kim Cattrall 2004

Mr Chow's restaurant in Beverly Hills is the place to find celebrities having dinner. I find it very strange that a lot of celebs go to these hotspots on a daily basis when they know there are going to be autograph collectors and photographers every single night. On this particular night, Al Pacino arrived at about 7pm, John Cleese arrived at 7:20pm and Kim Cattrall arrived at 7:40pm. When a star like Pacino arrives at Mr Chow's, a huge crowd of autograph collectors, mostly autograph sellers, somehow hear about it and within half an hour about 50 people are waiting outside the restaurant for him to leave.

When television star Kim arrived at the restaurant on this particular night she wouldn't stop for photos or autographs, but when she left all of the autograph collectors went for her. She tried to sign a few but was escorted to her waiting car. As she was being pushed and shoved I positioned myself so I could walk next to her. I asked her for a quick photo, my friend (God bless him) was waiting directly in front of us. I asked her to look at the camera and when she did my friend snapped this photo. It was chaos, something like you would see in a movie. Everyone was shoving photos in her face and screaming at her to sign her name. Every time she signed her name on a photo someone was making $50 to $100 from the sale of her autograph.

Larry King 2004

I first met television host Larry in 1999 outside a restaurant in LA called Spago's. Spago's used to be the place for the celebs to dine on a nightly basis. When I met him in 1999 he gave me a photo and asked me about Australia. When we finished speaking there was a homeless man standing nearby. Larry walked over to the guy and gave him a handful of money.

I met him again at Spago's in 2004 and he had not changed. He was generous with his time and once again gave me a photo. Maybe I should have asked him for a few dollars.

Ervin 'Magic' Johnson 2004

I had met Magic in Sydney in the mid 1990s and found
him to be very rude. I spent a few days trying to get
an autograph or a photo with the former LA Lakers
basketball great but he simply ignored me and all of
the other fans who were waiting for him. The only time
I saw him being friendly was when a television crew
was at his hotel and he walked over to a few young
kids and signed some autographs for them.

In 2004 I was in LA at a pre-Grammy's dinner. I was
having a really successful night as I had met about ten
different celebs. As the night was drawing to an end
I noticed Magic leaving the venue. All of the other
waiting autograph collectors had gone home, so I
walked up to him and asked for a photo. He told me
that he wasn't going to stop but I could have one with
him as he was walking. My friend snapped the photo
and I finally got what I had tried for about ten years
earlier.

Michael Stipe 2004

I first met Michael in Sydney in 1994 when REM was touring Australia. Back then he refused to sign autographs for anyone but agreed to photos with fans. Ten years on I was in LA at Mr. Chow's restaurant waiting with a few other fans to see what celebs we could meet. On this particular night I noticed Michael walk out of the restaurant and was waiting for his car to be dropped off by the valet. I am a bit of an REM fan and I instantly knew that it was Michael hiding behind the beard, hat and leather gloves.

I calmly walked up to him and asked for a photo. Very quietly he said to me that it was fine. After I had the photo taken with him the other guys who were waiting for autographs asked me who he was. When I told them they and a few photographers ran over to him, but he was already getting into his car. You have to be really on the ball—a split second could mean a missed opportunity.

P Diddy 2004

The first time I saw musician/clothing mogul P Diddy was when I was in LA in 2003. I was with my girlfriend in Beverly Hills doing the tourist thing when we noticed about ten huge guys surrounding P Diddy. Trailing behind them were three very large SUV cars. The whole street stopped as Diddy was doing a bit of shopping. I tried to walk up to him so I could ask for a photo, but as I approached him he got out his phone and pretended to talk on it. His bodyguards told me to not bother him as he was on the phone. He wasn't really on the phone—this is a trick that celebs use so the public don't approach them.

The next year I was back in LA dropping a photo off to a lady who worked in a hotel in Beverly Hills. When I walked into the hotel's lobby I noticed Diddy by himself in his socks on the house phone. When he got off the phone I asked for a photo with him. In a very quiet and shy voice he said, 'OK'. After the photo I said to him that he should come to Australia to do a tour as he had a lot of fans there. In his quiet and shy voice he said, 'Yeah I'd love to come to Australia for a tour.' Then the lift door opened and four of his huge bodyguards got out, they 'secured the area' and took their boss back in the lift.

I almost felt sorry for him, he had obviously just gone downstairs to make a simple phone call and his security team panicked and surrounded him. What a strange way to live.

Pamela Anderson 1995

Pamela Anderson 2004

I first tried for a photo with Pamela in 1995 when she was in Sydney for a music award show. Because of her security I wasn't able to get a photo with her, although I did take some of her while she was posing for the press on one of Sydney's beaches.

When I was in LA in 2004 a friend of mine told me that every morning Pamela goes to Starbucks in Malibu before she drops her kids to school. I drove to Malibu one morning to see if this was true. At about 8am I noticed Pamela walk into Starbucks and order a drink. I walked outside and waited for her to leave. When she did I asked her for a photo, and to my surprise she agreed.

It was one of those photos that people always take a second look at because they usually don't believe that it's Pamela Anderson. It always takes a few seconds for people to say, 'Oh I see it, oh my God! How different does she look without her make-up on.' That's why I love the photo so much. It shows people what celebs look like in real life.

Paula Abdul 2004

Once you're a celebrity in America you're always a celebrity in America. I have found that out because of my frequent trips to the States. Every time I turn on the televsion in America I see a celebrity who is long forgotten in every other country except for America. When one door closes another door opens. This saying is even truer today with reality TV. The last time I had heard of singer Paula Abdul was in about 1990 when she had a hit song called 'Opposites Attract'. Then in 2002 I saw Paula on television as a judge on American Idol.

I met her outside Mr Chow's restaurant in LA in 2004. She told me that she was supposed to come to Australia in the 1990s but at the last minute her record company cancelled the promo visit. She added that she had always wanted to come to Australia and hoped that one day she could make it down for a promo visit.

Don't get me wrong, she was very kind and sweet but if you really want to travel somewhere can't you just pay for your own ticket and have a holiday? Do celebs only visit other countries when they need to promote something and get all of their expenses paid for by the promotional companies? Let's hope she has another hit song so she can make it to Australia and anywhere else she wants to go!

Peter Falk 2004

As a kid I used to watch Peter in the hit television show *Colombo*. In 1990 he came to Sydney to film a TV commercial. I didn't know where he was staying so I wasn't able to meet him. In 2004 I was in LA and at a small café style restaurant in a hotel in Beverly Hills. When I sat down I noticed Peter Falk with his wife and a few seats down was Dennis Hopper. I had met Hopper in Sydney in 2002 so I didn't need a photo with him but I really wanted to get Peter.

I was told by a few autograph collectors that Peter doesn't really do a lot of photos and he can be difficult sometimes so I had to choose my words very carefully. I thought of a plan and went for it. I got up and went to the toilet. When I came back to my seat I walked past Peter and pretended that I had just noticed him. I introduced myself and told him that in 1990 when he was doing the ad in Sydney I was on the set as a work experience kid. I told him how kind he was to me on set and that I didn't have a camera with me in 1990.

The story put a smile on his face and he told me about his time spent in Sydney. I then said to him that I had told a bunch of friends that I was on set with him for the ad but because I never got a photo with him in 1990 no-one believed me. He then asked me if I had my camera with me. I replied, 'You know because I'm on holidays I do have my camera with me.' He said we'd better get a few photos so I could shut my friends up. He was in such a good mood that he asked me to take a photo of him with the waitress. When I dropped off the photo the next day to the waitress I bumped into P Diddy in the hotel foyer. It's so strange sometimes how I get to meet some of these celebrities.

Peter Jackson and Elijah Wood 2004

I went to the pre-BAFTA Awards luncheon in LA in 2004. The luncheon was held at a hotel just out of Beverly Hills and it was extremely easy to meet the celebs who had turned up for the day. When the luncheon had finished most of the people gathered in the hotel's foyer for a chat. I noticed writer/director Peter Jackson speaking with actor Elijah Wood *(The Lord of the Rings)*.

Just before they separated I asked them both if I could have a photo with them. Peter was a little hesitant about doing the photo but Elijah didn't care. I quickly reminded Peter that we were neighbours as he is a New Zealander and I'm an Aussie. That sealed the deal for me.

After the photo a few other people asked them but I was the only one who got it. It's a funny photo because the hair from the person behind me makes me look like I've got some hair growing up from the back of my head.

Ralph Lauren 2004

It was two days before New Year's Eve and fashion legend Ralph Lauren was in Sydney to see in the New Year. I received a phone call from a photographer friend of mine saying that Ralph was having dinner at Bondi Beach. I rang a few friends but nobody wanted to go with me to try to meet him. I arrived at the restaurant and was told by a waiting photographer that when Ralph and his friends arrived at the restaurant he was told by Ralph's security not to take any photos of the fashion mogul. The photographer left soon after I got there so I knew that I had a good chance of getting a photo with him.

When he did leave the restaurant I waited for him to have a chat with his friends about what they were going to do the next day, and when he was just about to walk to his car I politely said to him, 'Mr Lauren, I'm a great admirer of yours. I wear your clothes and fragrance [all true]. Would you do me the honour of letting me have my photo taken with you?' Ralph put out his hand and shook mine, thanked me for the compliment and gave me this photo.

Regis Fieldman 2004

I was waiting outside Mr Chow's restaurant in LA in 2004 when television star Regis and funny guy Martin Short left the restaurant together. I had a photo taken with Regis, then as I was getting a photo with Martin Short, Regis yelled out to him to come over to where he was as a mutual friend of theirs was waiting in a car to say hello. After Martin gave me the photo he was walking to the side of the road when Regis yelled out to him, 'Hurry up! It's Steve Martin in the car.'

I followed him over to a white car where Steve Martin was sitting in the driver's seat. As fate had it Steve Martin was driving past as his two friends were leaving Chow's. I waited for the three of them to have a chat and then asked Steve if I could have a photo with him. He said, 'I don't think so,' and then drove off. It's always so annoying when you have the chance to ask a celebrity for a photo and you're turned down. I would rather not have met them at all.

Scarlett Johansson 2004

When I got this photo with Scarlett in early 2004 I had no idea who she was. I was in LA at the pre-BAFTA Awards luncheon when my girlfriend noticed Scarlett leaving the luncheon. My girlfriend suggested that I get a photo with Scarlett as she was going to be the next 'big thing' to make it in Hollywood. Now the last time my girlfriend suggested I have a photo taken with someone that was going to be the next 'big thing' in Hollywood I ignored her advice. It turned out to be Angelina Jolie! I still kick myself!

I approached Scarlett for the photo but was surprised when she turned my request down. I then used my standard 'I'm from Australia and I probably won't be able to ever meet you again' line. Scarlett told me that there seemed to be a lot of foreigners around. I replied, 'Well, we're at an international hotel.' She instantly apologised and gave me the photo. I don't know what she'd be like to meet today after her rise to fame.

Shannen Doherty 2004

When I was in LA in 2004 I went to get some dinner at a restaurant/diner called, Johnny Rockets in Beverly Hills. Halfway through dinner I saw actor Shannen Doherty and her parents walking in. I finished my meal and walked over to say hello. The restaurant was empty so it was just Shannen, her mum and dad and my friend and girlfriend. As soon as she realised that we were from Australia her face lit up. 'I've always wanted to go to Australia,' she told us. I said, 'Well, you could have when you were dating Julian McMahon.' (Julian McMahon is a television star in the US and his father was the former Prime Minister of Australia.)

Shannen then invited the three of us to sit down and have a chat with her and her parents. We all introduced ourselves and the conversation started with Shannen telling us a story about Lady Sonia McMahon (Julian's mum). 'I was having a BBQ at my house when Julian and I were going out and his mum came to my house for the BBQ. When the food was served his mum refused to get off from her chair and get the food like everyone else. Instead she got Julian to get her food for her and bring it to her like she was better than the rest of us.'

I then told her not to worry as Lady Sonia had been pulled over by the police in Sydney for drink driving so she shouldn't think she was better than anyone else. That made everyone laugh. The night went so well that after our chat with Shannen she gave us her phone number because my friend was just about to open a restaurant in Australia and she said that she would love to come out for the opening. Shannen didn't come out for the opening due to her filming schedule, but that didn't bother us—we'd had a great night with the Dohertys.

Sidney Poitier 2004

Screen legend Sidney Poitier was the very first African–American male to win an Academy Award for best actor in 1963 for his starring role in *Lilies of the Field*. Now, this is a photo that I had been trying to get since the first time I went to LA in 1994. I asked everyone I knew in LA how I could meet Sidney. People told me that he went to a restaurant in Beverly Hills called Spago's at least once a week for dinner. At ever opportunity when I was in LA I waited at Spago's for Sidney but I never saw him. I was then told by a photographer that he has lunch and hangs out at a restaurant in Beverly Hills a few times a week. I checked it out but never saw him.

In 2004 when I was in LA I went to a pre-Grammy's function at a hotel in Beverly Hills. As the night finished the celebrities all waited in a long line for their cars. Just as my friend and I were about to leave he said to me, 'Sidney Poitier is behind you.' Now, my friend knew how much I wanted to meet Sidney so I thought that he was having a joke with me. I pretended to play it cool and didn't turn around, then Sidney walked passed me. I quickly followed and asked for a photo with him. Sidney kindly turned around and gave me the photo. It's so strange when you try to meet a celebrity for a number of years and then when you finally do it's over in seconds.

Sofia Coppola 2004

I met producer/writer Sofia Coppola in 2004 when
I was at the Beverly Hilton Hotel. A function had
finished in the hotel ballroom and a few celebs had
gone down to the pool area to do interviews. I went
down to the pool and pretended that I was a hotel
guest so I could fool the hotel's security; they were
throwing autograph collectors out of the hotel.

   After relaxing by the pool for a while I got a photo
with Sofia after she had finished her media obligations.

Stevie Wonder 2004

I had wanted to meet musician Stevie Wonder ever
since I started meeting international celebs in 1989,
but he had not been to Sydney since the mid 1980s.
So when I was in LA in 2004 and I saw him walking
towards Mr Chows restaurant I was extremely excited.
I asked him and his minder if I could please have a
photo with Stevie. His minder told me that I could but
asked if I could give them a minute. I waited as the
minder checked that Stevie looked okay for a photo.

After a few seconds I got the nod from his minder
to come over and get a photo, which I did. I then told
Stevie that he had a lot of fans in Australia who were
waiting for him to come and tour. He told me that he
would get down there soon. If and when Stevie does
tour Australia I can go to the show without the pressure
of thinking about whether I am going to get the photo
with him after the gig.

Anna Nicole Smith 2005

Anna Nicole came to Sydney in 2005 as a co-presenter of the 2005 Australian MTV Awards. I waited for her to come back to her hotel on the night of the awards. When she arrived at the hotel there were about eight fans waiting for her. As soon as she saw her fans she walked straight over to them and did practically anything that was asked of her.

At one stage her friend told her that she had spent enough time with the fans and told her to come into the hotel, but Anna Nicole was excited by the attention and she stayed a little longer. I was the last one to have a photo with her; it was worth the wait.

Billie Joe Armstrong 2005

I waited for Green Day band member Billie to come back from the 2005 Australian MTV Awards after party. At the hotel there were eight fans waiting to meet The Osbournes, Anna Nicole Smith and Green Day. I'm not a fan of their music, but when Billie arrived at the hotel I went up to him first and asked him for a photo. He said that it was fine but all the other fans were busy with their cameras and items for autographing. I had a digital camera so I took it myself.

Carmen Electra 2005

Actor Carmen Electra was in Sydney in 2005 for the Australian MTV Awards. I went to the press conference and when it finished I went backstage to the VIP area. Much to the dislike of the PR and security people I had a photo taken with Carmen. You should have seen the looks on their faces! The following year they had four security guards at the entrance and exit.

Kris Kristofferson 2005

I've said it once and I'll say it again, I love to meet the legends. They're much more important than a lot of today's so-called celebrities. I first met actor/singer Kris when he was in Sydney in 1991 with fellow country music greats Johnny Cash, Waylon Jennings and Willie Nelson. I missed out on getting a photo with him in 1991 so when I bumped into him in 2005 I was blown away.

    I had just had my first book released, *Australian Legends: People whose story we should know*, and the photos from the book were being exhibited in a hotel in Sydney. As I was showing a friend of mine my exhibition I noticed Kris having a look at my photos; he was staying in the hotel. I introduced myself and he gave me this photo.

Sean Connery 2005

Big screen Bond legend Sean Connery was in Sydney in 2005 for some business meetings. I received a phone call from a photographer friend of mine telling me that he had just photographed Sean entering a restaurant. I quickly grabbed a poster and camera and went to the restaurant. There were about 12 hired cars waiting outside the restaurant for Sean and his business companions. After waiting about an hour a limousine driver came up to me for a chat. He told me that he was the main driver of the limousines and that he was driving a famous Hollywood star. I pretended to not know who he was driving so I played a long with him. After a few more minutes of bragging the driver told me that he was driving Sean Connery.

'Sean Connery!' I replied in a surprised voice. 'Yes, that's right, the Sean Connery, I drive a lot of the big time celebrities,' replied the driver. As Sean was about to leave the restaurant I got my poster out of my bag. The driver saw me doing this and panicked. As Sean was walking out of the restaurant the driver grabbed my poster and tried to rip it out of my hand. I warned him to let the poster go; he had no choice as he had to drive Sean and his wife back to their hotel.

I got into my car and because I knew where he was staying I beat them back to the hotel. Once inside the lobby the driver ran up to me and said, 'Look, I don't know how you found out about all of this but you have to go.' I played it cool and when Sean entered the hotel he walked up to me and signed my poster. I then had this photo taken with him. I haven't seen the limousine driver before or after this night so I'm curious to know what other big celebrities he drives around.

Ozzy, Kelly and Jack Osbourne 2005

The Osbournes were in Sydney in 2005 to host the Australian MTV Awards. Kelly Osbourne was given two toy koalas as props for the press conference. After the press conference I waited at the side of the stage for the celebs to walk off. Ozzy, Kelly and Jack walked off first, leaving mum Sharon posing with Anna Nicole Smith and Carmen Electra for the media. I rounded the three of them up and my friend and I had a photo taken with them. The security was focused on the girls onstage, which made my life much easier.

Ashley Simpson 2006

Singer Ashley Simpson was in Sydney to be the presenter of the 2006 Australian MTV Awards At
the press conference she was given an MTV award, which is a platypus holding a surfboard.

A friend of mine told me that the Rolling Stones were also in Sydney and had a booking at a restaurant. I went down to
see if I could meet the Stones but they never showed up. Instead Ashley turned up for a booking. I asked her for a photo just
before she went into get a bite to eat.

Bob Geldof 2006

Bob was in Sydney in 2006 as part of his Australian tour. I met him at the airport when he arrived and I had this photo taken with him. The photo is unusual for two reasons: First, I am wearing an INXS T-shirt (which Bob didn't say anything about) and second, I had a magazine in my hand with Bob on one side and Michael Hutchence on the other.

   Bob signed his photo and I had this photo taken with him. Little did I know I folded the magazine in half just before the photo. I'm probably lucky that Bob didn't notice the photo of Michael because let's just say they didn't see eye to eye.

Bono 2006

Bono is not only the most famous rock star in the world but he is probably the most famous person in the world. I met Bono again in 2006 when U2 were on tour in Australia. Because he was staying in a house while he was in Sydney I had to try to meet him at the venue. My friend, who is a Beatles collector, has John Lennon's original 1968 Ivor Novello Award for the Beatles' song 'Hey Jude'. Bono arrived at the venue with a police escort, his car stopped and Bono opened the door. There were about 20 other fans waiting for Bono.

I positioned myself so I could get the award to Bono. Once I did Bono asked who the award belonged to, I told him that it was my friend's. Bono asked to meet my friend. The security held everyone back while my friend and I showed Bono the award. Bono is a huge John Lennon fan so he was very impressed. He gave us both a photo and posed with the award. For the next two gigs in Sydney Bono stopped his car when he arrived at the venue and signed autographs for every fan waiting for him, which on the last day was about 100 people. He spends time with his fans at every opportunity. Now that's a star!

Borat 2006

Sacha Baron Cohen, the man behind the characters Borat and Ali G, was in
Sydney in 2006 to promote his movie *Borat's Cultural Learning Of America For Make
Benefit Glorious Nation Of Kazakhstan*. When I arrived at the press conference I was told by the PR girls
that if I had any questions for Borat I would have to write them on a piece of paper and they would show them to him before
the press conference began. This gave me an insight into the way Sacha prepares his answers to the media's questions.

I always thought that his character was spontaneous. I had this photo taken with him just after the press conference was over.
Afterwards I noticed rapper/singer Kanye West walking past and I had a photo taken with him too. Two photos in two minutes—
it was almost like LA.

Chris Martin 2006

Chris and his band Coldplay were in Sydney in 2006 for a concert tour. I waited with two friends for Chris to arrive back at his hotel after one of their shows. Within an hour of them coming off stage Chris arrived. When he got there we walked up to him and he gave me a photo and signed some autographs for my friends.

    The funny thing was that when the other members of the band arrived at the hotel a few minutes later none of us knew their names so my friends couldn't get their autographs. Maybe we should have done a bit of research.

Jane Fonda 2006

Jane was in Sydney in 2006 to promote her autobiography *My Life*. Jane did an autograph signing at a book store in the city. After she signed books, photos, posters and anything else that the public asked her to sign, I asked if I could have a photo taken with her. I didn't want to stand in front of the table where she was sitting, I wanted to go behind the table so I could get a proper photo with her. Jane was really cool about my request adding, 'Well, you look pretty harmless to me.' She told the security that it was fine to let me go behind the desk and get the photo. For such a huge star she was very easy to meet.

Jessica on a boat on Sydney Harbour.

Jessica Simpson 2006

I went to the Hilton Hotel for the 2006 Australian MTV Awards press conference, which Jessica's sister Ashley was the star of. After the press conference most of the media gathered in the hotel foyer to see if Ashley and Jessica would go out together. I was in the lobby talking with some fans when I noticed singer Jessica and her parents talking about how they were going to exit the hotel without the media knowing.

I walked over to her and waited for the conversation to finish, and as I was waiting about seven photographers spotted her and started taking photos of them. Jessica and her parents walked back over to the lifts to avoid the photographers. As they were waiting for the lift I said, 'Jessica I'm a fan, can I please have my photo taken with you?' To her credit she asked me to come over to her and a friend of hers took this photo for me.

Nicole Kidman 2006

A photographer friend of mine called me with a tip-off that Nicole was hosting a special screening of the movie *Happy Feet* for sick children. I had tried to get her autograph a few times over the years but she either leaves a venue via the back door or simply turns down your request. Nicole is definitely one of the hardest celebrities to meet. When I arrived at the movies I noticed that I was the only person waiting for an autograph as it was not a publicised event, although all the media were informed.

When she arrived I asked her if she would be kind enough to sign a movie poster for me. If looks could kill I would be dead, but they don't so Nicole walked over to me and pretended to sign her name. This is a trick that the celebrities do so the media and the public take note that a star is signing for the fans—it's basically good PR for the celebrity. After she signed the poster I looked at it; she'd simply scribbled NK…I think that's what it says. I sometimes wish that they wouldn't sign anything at all if they are going to ruin your item, which in this case was an extremely rare 1980s Australian movie poster; very hard to get these days. Still, beggars can't be choosers.

Snoop Dogg 2006

My friend's child is a huge Snoop Dogg fan so when he came to Sydney for some concerts in 2006 I was asked by my friend's 11-year-old child if I could take her to meet rapper Snoop. We waited at the airport for half the day, then we found out that he had a private plane. I made a phone call and found out where he was staying. At the hotel we waited another five hours until we saw him. When we did he was surrounded by the biggest bodyguards I had ever seen and trust me I've seen some very big bodyguards over the years.

Snoop is 1.9 metres tall and two of his bodyguards were about a foot taller than him. We both stood up and I asked Snoop and his bodyguards if my friend's child could please have a photo with him. He just nodded his head to give us the all clear, the bodyguards moved away and my friend's child got to meet her idol. After she had the photo taken with him I got mine. If I look a little scared in the photo it's because I was.

Tyra Banks 2006

Beautiful model Tyra Banks was in Sydney in December 2006 to do some filming for her TV show *America's Next Top Model*. I had read in the press that she was difficult and that she was having problems with the local photographers. Early one morning a friend of mine called me telling me that Tyra was filming her show at a Sydney beach. I thought that I would go down and have a look. I picked up my friend's child, who is a huge Tyra fan, and drove to the beach. As we arrived on the beach Tyra was walking in our direction. We both stopped walking and waited for Tyra to walk over to us. Just as she got near us her bodyguard told us not to approach her for photos or autographs.

We just stood there looking at Tyra. The next thing we knew Tyra was walking over to us with a big smile and asked, 'Would you guys like a photo?' She then asked if she could have a look at my camera as she suggested that we use fill flash for the photo to get a better shot of the beach. Tyra then went through all the programmes on my camera to try to find the fill flash button. After a minute or two she couldn't find the flash button so we took the photos with this background instead of the water. My autograph friends in the US tell me that she is hard to get, but I found her to be one of the nicest celebrities I have met. I do wonder though if I would've got the photo with her if I didn't have a child with me.

Adam West and Burt Ward 2007

This is the very first photo that I have ever had to pay the actual celebrity for. While I was in LA in 2007 I went to an autograph show. When I arrived I saw about 100 or so celebrities sitting behind tables. I walked around and noticed that you had to pay the celebrity for an autograph and a photo with them. I was mainly after a photo not an autograph, and I asked Burt Ward (Robin) and Adam West (Batman) if I could have my photo in between them. Burt said it was fine but I had to pay him $30. I then asked Adam, who told me to ask his manager. His manager told me that Adam doesn't do photos and autographs because people sometimes forge his autograph from the original and use the photo to try and sell his autograph on eBay.

Because I was only after a photo I was able to get one in between them both. While I was standing in between them Adam was speaking to a fan and the line to meet them both was growing. Burt said to Adam, 'Sir Batman, could you stop talking so we can get this photo done.' Adam faced the camera and my friend snapped the photo. It cost me $60 dollars and Adam isn't even looking at the camera. Kapow!

Billy Crystal 2007

Comedian/actor Billy Crystal was in Sydney in early 2007 for his one man show *700 Sundays*. I took this photo of him at his Sydney press conference. After the press conference one of the photographers quickly made his way over to Billy and asked for his autograph. I took this opportunity to get out my poster and have it signed. The media started to get a bit restless and one photographer yelled out, 'What is this, Billy? An autograph session or a photo call?' Billy ignored the comment and signed a few more autographs.

Clint Eastwood 2007

One night in LA I got a tip-off that Clint was going to be given an award at the Beverly Hilton Hotel to celebrate his achievements in cinema. He was to arrive at the hotel via the loading dock. After waiting outside in the freezing cold for two hours I decided to go into the hotel to see if I could see any sign of him. Dressed in a suit and tie I waited for about 45 minutes in the hotel lobby. From out of nowhere a side door opened and out walked Clint with a security guard from the hotel. I walked up to him and asked if I could have my photo taken with him. He told me that he couldn't do anything in the hotel but suggested that I walk outside with him.

Once outside, Clint was approached by about ten autograph collectors. Clint said, 'Oh I didn't realise there was so many people waiting outside.' He than added that because he was holding a very heavy award he couldn't stop for autographs and photos. The fans, including myself, kept asking him to. He then said, 'Let me put this award in the car and I will sign for you guys.' He got to the car and told the fans that he would sign one autograph per person. My friend and I stood behind him near his car while he was standing on the footpath signing. He said to my friend that he thought that one autograph had now become three, adding, 'Don't worry, I won't forget about you guys from Down Under.'

After a few minutes of signing autographs Clint got in the car and told my friend and I to get our photos with him. Then for some unknown reason the security guard that had been silent the entire time told Clint that he shouldn't give us a photo and tried to close the car door. Clint told the guy that it was okay. I took the first photo for my friend, but when I wanted my photo taken the security guard tried his very best to push me away from the car. I told him that Clint had said it was fine to have my photo taken with him, but for some reason this guy was on a power trip.

Once again he tried to slam the car door shut, the only problem being that I was standing there. Again Clint told the guy to allow me to have my photo with him. I stood my ground. As I was getting the photo the security guard had his hand on me trying his very best to pull me from the photo. It's an awkward photo that should have taken only a few seconds, but because of a power hungry security guard it took a lot longer with unnecessary drama. Maybe the guy was trying to audition for one of Clint's movies as an overprotective power hungry idiot.

Eddie Murphy 2007

In LA you can literally bump into celebrities everywhere you go. I had just arrived at a hotel in Beverly Hills one night when my friend told me that Eddie was out the front of the hotel with about 20 other people waiting for their cars. I positioned myself so I was standing next to him and asked Eddie for a photo. He kindly posed for me and then for my friend, but when I looked at my photo I noticed that it was blurry. I stood next to him again and told him that my photo didn't turn out. I asked him again if I could please get another one, but just as I was about to get it the doorman from the hotel started yelling at me telling me that I was not allowed to get a photo with Eddie.

I tried to explain to him that Eddie agreed to my request, but the guy yelled at me for about 40 seconds. When he stopped to take a breath Eddie said to me that I better get the photo before he started yelling at me again. The whole event should have taken two seconds but because the hotel's doorman lost his cool it took a lot longer. In contrast Eddie couldn't have been more cool about it.

Georgio Armani 2007

I had arrived at Mr Chow's restaurant in LA one night to find about 50 or so photographers, videographers and autograph collectors all waiting out the front. I knew that there had to be a big name inside. I was told by some people that Australians Nicole Kidman, Keith Urban, Hugh Jackman, Deborra-Lee Furness and Rupert Murdoch were all inside having dinner together. I was also told that fashion legend Georgio Armani was inside the restaurant.

The Australians left first, which cut the people waiting out the front by half. When Armani left about 15 people tried for an autograph and a further ten or so started taking photos. Armani had two bodyguards either side of him. My friend and I told him that we were from Australia and asked if we could have a photo with him while his security was escorting him to his car.

As luck would have it, his assistant whispered in his ear in Italian that we were from Australia and we wanted a photo with him. He instantly turned around, gave us both a smile and put his arm out for a photo. He was such a nice guy that I felt like buying one of his suits. Then I looked at my bank balance and thought I'd make do with the photo.

Helen Mirren 2007

I was told by a friend that actor Helen Mirren was to be the special guest at a dinner to be held in her honour at a hotel in Beverly Hills. I put on a suit and casually waited in the foyer of the hotel. After about 30 minutes Helen walked passed me. I got up from from my chair and introduced myself. I told her that a friend of mine in Australia by the name of Michael Pate directed or produced the movie *Age of Consent* (1969) in which Helen co-starred. Helen replied, 'No it was Michael Powell.'

Now, I was convinced that Michael Pate directed or produced the movie so I say, 'No it was Michael Pate.' Helen replies, 'No it was Michael Powell who directed the movie'. I then say, 'We are speaking of Norman Lindsay's *Age of Consent* aren't we?' 'Yes,' replied Helen. At this stage of the conversation I am regretting bringing up the movie, director and producer. I asked for a photo with her, and she kindly consented. I did some research and found out that Michael Pate was the associate producer of *Age of Consent* and Michael Powell was the director. I was close.

Heroes 2007

Hayden Panettiere, Noah Gray-Cabey, Greg Grunberg

It's my third day in LA and I'm asked by a friend of mine in Sydney to go to a press conference to take some photos of any celebrities who attend. The press conference is to gain some media exposure to help save the whales from getting slaughtered around the world. When I arrive at the venue a young girl introduced herself as Hayden. I thought she was part of the media so I ask her if any celebs had arrived. Hayden tells me that a few of her cast mates were casually walking around, 'Cast mates?' I ask. 'Yes,' replied Hayden, 'I'm in a show called *Heroes*.'

Embarrassed, I tell her that *Heroes* had only just started in Australia the week that I left for LA and I hadn't seen any episodes. Hayden was really cool and introduced my friend and I to her fellow cast mates Noah Gray-Cabey (young boy) and Greg Grunberg. After the press conference I asked Hayden if she would pose for a photo for me. She happily agreed and we did a few photos before she was whisked off to do some more filming for the hit television show *Heroes*.

Jack Nicholson 2007

Jack is a huge LA Lakers basketball fan so when I was in LA in January 2007 I went to a Lakers game to see if I could meet him and any other celebs. Just before the game was to begin a stretch limo turned up and out got Jack. My friend and I asked him for a photo and Jack said that he would do it after the game. Within a few seconds of Jack leaving the game he was surrounded by about 15 autograph collectors. He happily signed autographs, but when we asked him for a photo he told us that he doesn't do photos with fans anymore.

I walked next to him and told him that I was from Australia and this would be my one and only chance to ever get a photo with him, but he repeated that he didn't do photos. Jack stood at his car and continued to sign autographs but would not give me or anyone else a photo with him. I tried to take one while I was standing next to him but he had his head down signing autographs. As he drove off a young fan yelled out to him and Jack leaned across the back of his car to shake the young fan's hand. I was disappointed that I actually got to stand next to him but couldn't get a photo with him. So close but yet so far!

Jack Nicholson 2007

One week after my meeting with Jack at a Lakers game I was waiting at Mr. Chow's restaurant. When I arrived my friend told me that Jack was inside. I was also told that he usually has a smoke out the back of the restaurant. Because there were over 30 photographers, videographers and autograph collectors all waiting for him out the front I figured that I may have a better chance of meeting Jack out the back if he decided to have a smoke.

After waiting out the back for about 30 minutes my friend and I noticed him walk out for a cigarette. We walked up to Jack and introduced ourselves and asked him if it would be possible to have a photo taken with him. Once again he told us that he didn't do photos. I then told him that had I tried to get a photo with him about a week ago at the basketball game, 'Oh yes I remember,' Jack replied. I then asked him if I could tell him a story. Jack took a puff of his cigarette and said, 'Sure you can.'

I then told him a true story about when he was in Sydney in 1998. I had met him at his hotel after he spent the day playing golf. He happily signed a poster for me but when I asked him for a photo with him he told me that he lost his glasses on the golf course, so without his trademark glasses he wouldn't do the photo. Jack looked at me and says, 'Yeah I remember losing my glasses on the golf course.' I then tell him that I had waited nine years for this opportunity to have my photo with him. He said he wasn't wearing any glasses at that moment either so he couldn't give me a photo.

I decided to get off the subject so I changed the conversation. My friend then asked Jack why he is so cool and why everyone else can't be like him. Jack jokingly replied, 'Then what am I going to do?' After ten minutes with us Jack finished his smoke and whispered in my ear, 'When I leave I will have my glasses on and I will give you the photo.'

An hour later I got a call telling me that Jack was out the front. My friend and I quickly ran around the front to find about 50 people all waiting. Flashes were going off, people were yelling his name and fans were trying to get his autograph. Jack then saw me and told me to come over to him. He put his arm around me and said, 'Let's do this photo.' After that he gave my friend one also, then got in his car and did nothing for anyone else. After he left a few people came up to me and told me that Jack was standing out the front of Chow's for about two minutes just looking at people. They thought that he was waiting to give us the photo before he left. You can tell by the look on my face that I am losing it—can you blame me? Jack Nicholson!

Jane Russell 2007

Hollywood legend Jane Russell was at an autograph convention when I was in LA in January 2007. When I arrived at the show I saw a line of about 15 people waiting to meet her. This was my very first time at one of these conventions so when it came time to meet her I noticed that I had to pay $30 dollars for an autograph and $20 for a photo with her. I told her that I was from Australia and that it was a huge honour for me to meet her. She then stopped signing her name and said, 'I'm sorry that I don't look like I used to.'

　　After having my photo taken with Jane she handed me the photo that she had signed. She then said, 'Tell me what I have written on the photo for you.' The photo was of Jane lying on a stack of hay with a gun in her hand from the 1943 movie *The Outlaw*. It read, 'Richard, I'd love to shoot you but I just can't get up, Jane Russell.'

Kirk Douglas 2007

When I travelled to LA in early 2007 I did so with a friend of mine who brought a car boot lid painted with Kirk's portrait all the way from Australia. My friend wanted Kirk to sign his art piece and hopefully get a photo with the Hollywood legend. We went to Kirk's known hang-outs while we were in LA but had no luck meeting him. On the very last day of our stay a friend took us on a drive through Hollywood and Beverly Hills.

As we were heading back to our hotel our friend drove us past Kirk's house, and we all noticed Kirk standing out the front having a chat with a neighbour. We stopped the car and my friend got his art piece out and showed Kirk, who liked the 'auto art' very much. Kirk happily signed it and posed for photos with the three of us.

Matt Lucas and David Walliams 2007

Little Britain is one of my all time favourite TV shows, so when the stars of the show Matt Lucas and David Walliams came to Sydney in early 2007 for a tour of their hit show I decided that I wanted to try to meet them and get a photo in between them. I waited at the airport for them to arrive and when they did I asked Matt if I could have my photo taken with the both of them. After they signed some autographs for a few waiting fans I got the group photo.

Martin Scorsese 2007

I arrived at Mr Chow's restaurant one night and was told that director Scorsese was inside but he went in through the back. My friend and I went to the back of the restaurant and found about ten fans waiting for his autograph. An hour or so later Scorsese left Chow's and started signing autographs. While he was happily signing, a lady from the restaurant came out the back and started screaming at the collectors not to get his autograph, to get back and not to approach him. Scorsese didn't seem to be bothered by signing for the collectors. In fact he had a huge smile on his face.

After a few minutes of him signing and this lady yelling, she took the pen from his hand and told him to get in his car. As he was walking to his waiting car I asked him if I could have a photo with him, adding that I was from Australia. The lady told him not to stop but Scorsese instantly turned around and told the lady that he would give me a photo as I was from Australia. To be honest I could have been from Mars and he still would have given me the photo, he was such a nice guy. What a pity that this over-protective lady had to be there to ruin the moment for everyone.

Michael Parkinson 2007

Michael was in Sydney in early 2007 as the presenter of *Symphony at the Movies*, which was held at the Sydney Opera House. After one of his performances I waited at the stage door for him to leave. I was surprised to find that I was the only one. After two hours of waiting Michael finally left through the stage door. I knew that his idol was Sir Donald Bradman and I also knew that even though he had met and interviewed some of the biggest names in the world he never got the chance to meet Sir Donald.

After I had my photo taken with him I showed him some photos of me with Hollywood legends like Audrey Hepburn and Gregory Peck. Michael flicked through the photos but didn't comment on any of them until he got to the very last one, which was a photo of me with Sir Donald Bradman. Michael looked at the photo for a few seconds and asked, 'How did you meet Sir Donald Bradman?' I told him that I met Sir Donald in 1995 and 1996 at his home in Adelaide when I photographed him for my first book. Michael looked at me and said, 'Well, you did more than I did.'

Nastassja Kinski and Jane Russell 2007

This photo shows that celebrities also collect autographs. I was at an autograph show in LA in January 2007 where I met everyone from the original Batman and Robin to Pee Wee Herman. At the end of the day I was having a chat with Hollywood legend Jane Russell when Nastassja Kinski, who was a celebrity autograph signer at the show, introduced herself to Jane. She told Jane that she was a huge fan and added that she would love to get an autograph.

Jane pulled out a photo of herself and asked Nastassja how to spell her name. Nastassja tried to spell it out to Jane but because Jane is in her mid-eighties she couldn't hear her properly. Nastassja was very embarrassed, but after a minute or two Jane dedicated and signed the photo. I then commented to Nastassja that now she knows what it's like to be on the other side of the table. After she got her autograph Nastassja was kind enough to pose for a photo with her newly acquired Jane Russell signature.

Nicollette Sheridan 2007

I took this photo in February 2007 outside Mr Chow's restaurant in Beverly Hills. *Desperate Housewives* star Nicollette Sheridan is trying to leave the restaurant with photographers and videographers surrounding her car. In the last couple of years I have noticed a huge change in the number of photographers and videographers in LA; it has tripled. I couldn't believe that when Nicollette got in her car some of the waiting media leaned on the front of her car and not only flashed her a number of times but a few of the videographers turned the lights on their video cameras and completely blinded her. Nicollette had to just sit in her car and wait for two of the restaurant workers to try to get the media away from the front of her car.

If this continues in LA (and it's getting worse every year) I'm sure that something serious is going to happen, either to one of the celebrities or to one of the media. The strange thing is that when someone like Nicollette visits Sydney she has at least two bodyguards with her and there may be one or two photographers waiting for her, but when she is in LA she has no bodyguards and there are dozens of photographers, videographers, etc.

However, celebrities continue going to these places knowing that there is going to be mayhem and then they complain about unwanted attention from the media when they are not working. If they don't want all the attention then why go to these restaurants where there is 20 or so photographers waiting outside the restaurant every night? As Cate Blanchett said in a 2006 interview, 'I absolutely accept that there's a public side to my job, but if you don't want to be seen, there are places you don't go.'

Peter O'Toole 2007

It's a few days out from the 2007 Academy Awards and a friend in LA tells me that actor Peter O'Toole has just checked into a hotel in Beverly Hills. My friend and I put on our suits and casually wait in the hotel lobby. There is three of the hotel's security in the lobby to try to catch any wandering autograph collectors or photographers. Because we are dressed in our suits and obviously have nothing to get signed we are safe—for about 30 minutes.

When I'm in a situation like this I always speak a little louder than I usually would so that the hotel staff knows that I am a foreigner. Within five minutes of waiting in the lobby, Peter walks in and gets straight into the lift. My friend and I follow. Once in the lift we pretend not to notice Peter, and play it cool until the doors open. All three of us get out of the lift and I introduce myself. I tell Peter a true story about how as a young adult my grandfather met Australia's very own Peter Finch. It turns out that Peter O'Toole and Peter Finch were the very best of friends. So after a short chat about 'Finchy' and him hanging out together many years ago, Peter allows me and my friend to have a photo taken with him. He was a true gentleman with a strong charisma.

Robert Downey Jr 2007

This photo just goes to show that I can't always get a photo with every celebrity that I try to meet. I arrived at Mr Chow's restaurant in Beverly Hills late one night only to find about 30 or so photographers, videographers and autograph collectors all standing out the front. I ask whose inside and I'm told a few names but the one that I really wanted was actor Robert Downy Jr. I became a fan of Robert's in 1992 when I saw the movie *Chaplin*. I was told that he is usually very nice and on the way in he stopped for autograph collectors and did a few photos for waiting fans. I ask how many people were out the front when he went in, I was told about ten.

When he came out of the restaurant he was swamped by the crowd that had gathered outside. Robert stood near the front doors of Chow's and waited for his car. When it arrived he quickly dashed to it and unfortunately I couldn't get a photo with him, because as he politely told me if he did one for me he would have to do one for everyone else. The night wasn't a complete loss though, as I did take this photo of him as he was waiting for his car. It's another one for the so-close-and-yet so far folder.

Ron Howard 2007

While I was in LA I found out that actor/director Ron Howard was going to be honoured at the 21ˢᵗ Annual American Society of Cinematographers Awards. I put on my suit and went into the hotel's ballroom where the ceremony was taking place. When the night had come to an end I went up to Ron and congratulated him on receiving the Board of Governors Award. He thanked me for the compliment and then gave me this photo with him, which I call 'The two bald and bearded guys'. There were a few other celebs in the room, the biggest being Charlize Theron, who wouldn't sign autographs or pose for photos with anyone in the room, telling people that it wasn't her night.

Sophia Loren 2007

For me, meeting a legend like Sophia Loren is far more important than meeting many of today's 'stars'. A legend will be remembered for many years to come, unlike most of today's plastic throw away disposable stars, who will only be remembered for leaving nightclubs drunk and checking in and out of rehab. Sophia came to Sydney in 2007 for the Italian film festival. I went to her press conference but couldn't get a photo with her because there were too many photographers. The next day my friend and I waited for her to arrive back at her hotel, when she did I showed her an original 1955 Life magazine that she was on the cover of, she just glanced at it and kept walking. Lucky for me my friend Grayem had a car boot lid which uniquely had Sophia's portrait painted on it. Sophia signed the portrait of her and then gave both of us a photo. A true legend and a very beautiful lady, can you believe in these two photos that she is seventy two? Amazing!

The Reverend Jesse Jackson 2007

I didn't think that I would see religious leader Reverend Jesse Jackson at a celebrity hang-out like Mr Chow's restaurant in Beverly Hills but lucky for me I did. When he arrived I asked him for a photo, as he turned around to give me the photo a group of ladies started to yell his name so he walked over in their direction and began to shake their hands. He then went into the restaurant without giving me the photo. I quickly went down the road to a hotel where Helen Mirren was getting honoured, and was lucky to get a photo with her. I went back to Chow's and had this photo taken with the Reverend Jackson, when he was leaving. What a night!

Zach Braff 2007

One of my favourite television shows of the past few years has been *Scrubs*. When I was at the LA Lakers basketball game in January 2007 I noticed Zach who plays Dr John 'JD' Dorian just outside the game having a chat with some friends. I waited until he was finished and asked him for a photo. He picked up my Australian accent and said to me, 'G'day, mate, how's it going?' After he gave me the photo a few other fans noticed him and he ended up spending about ten minutes posing for photos and simply hanging out with fans.

When it was time for him to leave, a homeless man asked him for some money. Zach gave the man $20 and asked him not to spend it on booze or smokes. I then jokingly asked him for some money to take back to Australia. We had a laugh and he came back over to me to shake my hand. What a nice guy!

Snap
Crackle
and Pop Art

ABOVE
Billie Joe Armstrong 2005-2006
RIGHT
Anna Nicole Smith 2005-2006

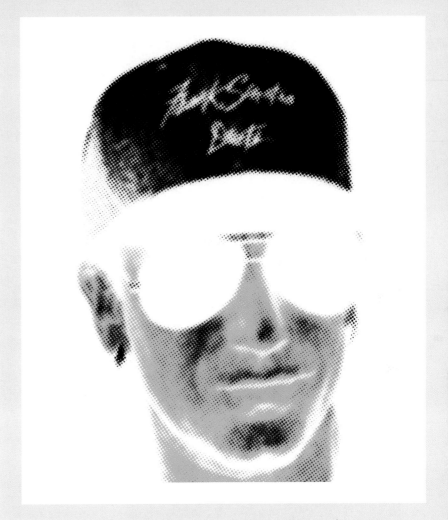

ABOVE
Bono 1993-2006

LEFT
Debbie Harry 1990-2006

Flea The Red Hot Chili Peppers

1992-2006

Iggy Pop

2006

ABOVE
Mel Gibson
2002-2006

ABOVE
Michael Hutchence
2002-2006

ABOVE
Mischa Barton
2006

ABOVE
Paris and Nikki Hilton
2003-2006

Thank you...

As you can imagine with a book like this there are a number of people to thank. If I've forgotten anyone and your name's not in this section then you can write it in yourself—I'll leave some room for you.

Thank you to my publishers for publishing my second book, with a very special thanks to Fiona Schultz and Martin Ford at New Holland. My love and thanks to Samara, Mum, Grayem, Miles, Danielle, Christy, Steve, Jason, Laura, Peter Carrette—Icon Images, Bob Sach—Lucky Mat, Patrick Riviere and Sylvie—Sydney Freelance, Bob King, Ben Mitchel, Nick, Linda, Kylie, Leanne, Dorothy, Howard, Adam, George, Michael, Katrina, Ellysha, Roger, Stephen Dupont, Katrina Ross, Yvette, Lana, Portia, Liz, Dave, Chris at Max's near the old Sebel, Frank, Glen, Jewels, Keith, Kent, Kristen, Salle, Scott, James, Steve (Glen's mate), Terry and Stella Coulits—Sydney Spinal Care, Tony, Joseph, Valerie, Angie, Todd, the Hutchence family, INXS, the staff at Rhinoceros Recording Studio (Sydney), David Keeler, Shannon, Lee and Bron, Jack 'Pa Pa' White, Todd, Rich 'Hollywood' Duma, Nick—UK, Gary Lee Boas, John—Perfection Chocolates, Christian 'Jo Jo' Mukendi, Gus, Luz, Dad and Uncle Paul.

PS. Thank you to all of those people over the years who have made my life, shall we say, a little harder by trying to stop me from having my photo taken with these celebrities. I hope you really enjoy this book and that these photos remind you of how you failed and I won!

Access All Areas…………Sometimes